The Gasconade Review presents:

# Missouri is a Ghost-Shaped Thing

Edited by John Dorsey and Jason Ryberg

Spartan Press
Kansas City, MO
spartanpresskc@gmail.com

Copyright © Jason Ryberg, 2018
First Edition 1 3 5 7 9 10 8 6 4 2
ISBN: 978-1-946642-50-9
LCCN: 2018940724

Design, edits and layout: Jason Ryberg,
Cover image, title page and exit images: Jamie Rhodes
All rights reserved. No part of this publication may be reproduced or transmitted in any form or by any means, electronic or mechanical, including photocopying, recording or by info retrieval system, without prior written permission from the author.

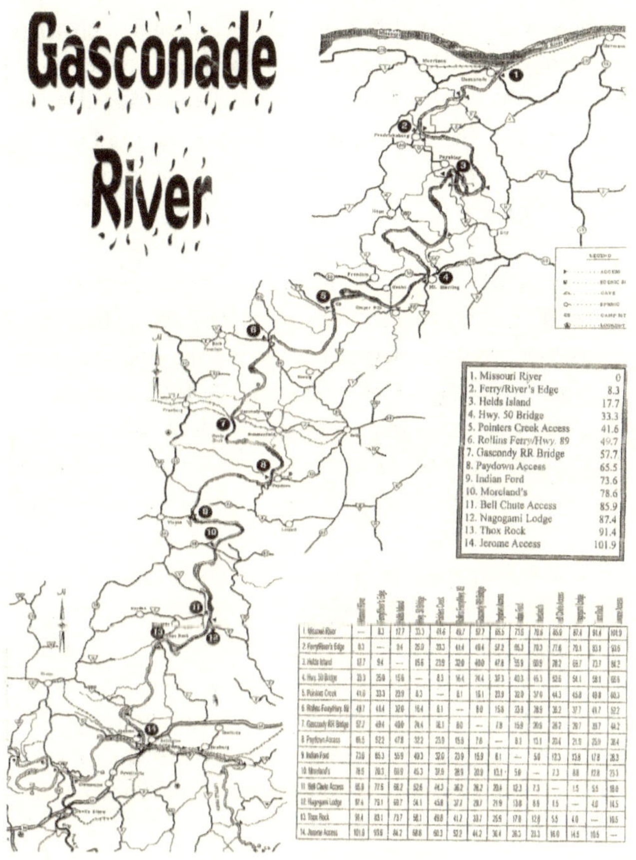


| | | | | | | | | | | | | | | |
|---|---|---|---|---|---|---|---|---|---|---|---|---|---|---|
| 1. Missouri River | — | 8.3 | 17.7 | 33.3 | 41.6 | 49.7 | 57.7 | 65.5 | 73.6 | 78.6 | 85.9 | 87.4 | 91.4 | 101.9 |
| 2. Ferry/River's Edge | 8.3 | — | 9.4 | 25.0 | 33.3 | 41.4 | 49.4 | 57.2 | 65.3 | 70.3 | 77.6 | 79.1 | 83.1 | 93.6 |
| 3. Helds Island | 17.7 | 9.4 | — | 15.6 | 23.9 | 32.0 | 40.0 | 47.8 | 55.9 | 60.9 | 68.2 | 69.7 | 73.7 | 84.2 |
| 4. Hwy. 50 Bridge | 33.3 | 25.0 | 15.6 | — | 8.3 | 16.4 | 24.4 | 32.3 | 40.3 | 45.3 | 52.6 | 54.1 | 58.1 | 68.6 |
| 5. Pointers Creek | 41.6 | 33.3 | 23.9 | 8.3 | — | 8.1 | 16.1 | 23.9 | 32.0 | 37.0 | 44.3 | 45.8 | 49.8 | 60.3 |
| 6. Rollins Ferry/Hwy. 89 | 49.7 | 41.4 | 32.0 | 16.4 | 8.1 | — | 8.0 | 15.8 | 23.9 | 28.9 | 36.2 | 37.7 | 41.7 | 52.2 |
| 7. Gascondy RR Bridge | 57.7 | 49.4 | 40.0 | 24.4 | 16.1 | 8.0 | — | 7.8 | 15.9 | 20.9 | 28.2 | 29.7 | 33.7 | 44.2 |
| 8. Paydown Access | 65.5 | 57.2 | 47.8 | 32.2 | 23.9 | 15.8 | 7.8 | — | 8.1 | 13.1 | 20.4 | 21.9 | 25.9 | 36.4 |
| 9. Indian Ford | 73.6 | 65.3 | 55.9 | 40.3 | 32.0 | 23.9 | 15.9 | 8.1 | — | 5.0 | 12.3 | 13.8 | 17.8 | 28.3 |
| 10. Moreland's | 78.6 | 70.3 | 60.9 | 45.3 | 37.0 | 28.9 | 20.9 | 13.1 | 5.0 | — | 7.3 | 8.8 | 12.8 | 23.3 |
| 11. Bell Chute Access | 85.9 | 77.6 | 68.2 | 52.6 | 44.3 | 36.2 | 28.2 | 20.4 | 12.3 | 7.3 | — | 1.5 | 5.5 | 16.0 |
| 12. Nagogami Lodge | 87.4 | 79.1 | 69.7 | 54.1 | 45.8 | 37.7 | 29.7 | 21.9 | 13.8 | 8.8 | 1.5 | — | 4.0 | 14.5 |
| 13. Thox Rock | 91.4 | 83.1 | 73.7 | 58.1 | 49.8 | 41.7 | 33.7 | 25.9 | 17.8 | 12.8 | 5.5 | 4.0 | — | 10.5 |
| 14. Jerome Access | 101.9 | 93.6 | 84.2 | 68.6 | 60.3 | 52.2 | 44.2 | 36.4 | 28.3 | 23.3 | 16.0 | 14.5 | 10.5 | — |

The **Gasconade River** is about 280 miles (450 km) long and is located in central and south-central Missouri in the United States. The Gasconade River begins in the Ozarks southeast of Hartville in Wright County and flows generally north-north-eastwardly through Wright, Laclede, Pulaski, Phelps, Maries, Osage and Gasconade counties, through portions of the Mark Twain National Forest. It flows into the Missouri River near the town of Gasconade in Gasconade County.

The name Gasconade is derived from "Gascon", an inhabitant of the French region of Gascony. The people of that province were noted for their boastfulness. It was applied by the early French to the Indians living on its banks who bragged about their exploits. The name means to boast or brag, and thus the river received its name. The waters of the river are boisterous and boastful and the name is also descriptive.

The headwaters of the Gasconade are in the southeastern corner of Webster County northeast of Seymour, Missouri where it drains the eastern margin of the Springfield Plateau at approximately 37°11'54"N 92°41'44"W. The river joins the Missouri River at the city of Gasconade at 38°40'28"N 91°32'55"W The river follows a meandering course through the Ordovician age dolostone and sandstone bedrock of the Ozark Salem Plateau creating spectacular bluffs and incised meanders along the way. Numerous springs and caves occur within the drainage area and along the river course. Significant tributaries include the Osage Fork of Webster and Laclede counties and Roubidoux Creek and Big Piney River of Texas and Pulaski counties. The Roubidoux and Big Piney flow respectively along the west and east boundaries of Fort Leonard Wood which lies a short distance south and east of the Gasconade.

The plateau surface near the midpoint is 300 feet (91 metres) above the river bottom near the river midpoint northeast of Waynesville creating scenic river bluffs. At the junction with the Missouri the river bottom is about 400 feet (120 m) lower in elevation than the old plateau surface above the river. The elevation of the plateau rim at the headwaters is at or above 1,600 feet (490 m) with local hilltops at over 1,700 feet (520 m) (second highest elevation in Missouri near Cedar Gap). The elevation at the confluence with the Missouri is 500 feet (150 m) giving an overall drainage basin relief of 1,200 feet (370 m).

It is ranked with a difficulty of I and II (seldom) by those who canoe, kayak and float. It is considered a good float stream because there's typically not a heavy congestion of boats. It is common to go for many miles without seeing another boat.

There are caves and an abundance of wildlife along the river and is considered a popular place by anglers for its largemouth bass and smallmouth bass.

The Gasconade River is the longest river completely within the boundary of Missouri. It has been called one of the world's crookedest rivers.

The **Gasconade Review** is a literary and arts publication based out of the Osage Arts Community (http://osageac.org/), located on the Gasconade River, just outside of Belle, Missouri. It appears twice annually, focusing primarily, but not exclusively, on writers and artists from the region and state, but occasionally also features *folks what ain't from around here.* All submissions must be hand delivered between the months of April and October and the hours of 3pm to 6pm. A decent bourbon is appreciated. Proper river attire required. Don't worry, the dogs won't bite.

*The Gasconade Review was created as part of Belle's Poet Laureate project at the beginning of 2017. Original founded as a means to showcase work by poets and artists from around the fine state of Missouri, our scope has since grown to include pieces from all over the American Midwest, and we're darn proud to be able to offer you the works in the volume you're currently holding in your hands.*

—John Dorsey, Founding Co-Editor and first Poet Laureate of Belle, 2017-2019

# CONTENTS

*They say Missouri is a ghost-shaped thing.*

-Chigger Matthews

*Barn* by Justin Hamm

## Scot Young

### the greatest generation goes to war

*--for dad*

tom brokaw said you were from the
greatest generation but you went 4F
instead of being inducted with yr brothers
instead of storming the beach at normandy...
the army said not acceptable for military service
you were not good enough
to be first to die when they dropped the ramp
the greatest generation didn't talk about the war
and your stories were never discussed
you disappeared for weeks on induction day
never dropped the ramp to hit the beach
or ever stopped to let others aboard
but spent next 50 odd years going 4F
drowning in the land of sky blue waters
most days after work wrapping
yourself around a can or bottle
trying to forget or was it
to remember?
every other saturday we would get a haircut
at joe's & stop in at the hangout bar  for a couple
you sat at the table when you had me
go along—wasn't right for a kid
to sit at a bar you'd say…

at age seven I asked you once
daddy what did you do in the war?
you swirled your beer in the glass
those blue eyes narrowed
looking right through me
drank it down
ordered another
asked me if i wanted another coke…
and don't tell your mother
we were here
they say you never ask
the greatest generation about the war
the ones that made it back will take
the stories to their grave
the ones that never made it
will do the same
every single day.

## sunday morning

buster
redbone hound
sleeps soundly
on the front porch
stretched out taking
in the morning sun
dreaming
of the next hunt
you are in the house
frying bacon
making scratch biscuits
maple flavor
drifts through
the open window
you sing streisand
it sounds good
paired against
these ozark hills
almost spiritual
bringing culture
to this holler
blue car stops
in driveway
jehovah's witness
steps out
begins the conversation

ol’ buster raises up
barks slightly
looks him straight
in the eye
and begins
licking his balls
like any good
coonhound
would do
on a perfect
sunday morning

## the jazz of milton morris

we held our union
meetings upstairs
but downstairs
at the tap room
milton morris sold
kansas city
jazz and juice
friend of basie
parker and young

and during prohibition
since both were illegal
he sold whiskey and reefer
25 cents
for medicinal purposes
only
but it was the jazz
that hooked you
the blue haze
& cool saxophone
drifting down main
like a lonely lady
in a red dress
lingering
selecting
a slow song
on the last
jukebox
ever made.

## Jonie McIntire

# Passing

The day my uncle hung himself in the backyard,
his sister sunbathing in the front, and his brother
spotting him just before the snap,
my father and I toured a college campus,
ate Ethiopian food with our fingers —
my father, always so tidy, humming
as sauce dripped, his pressed grey slacks
wrinkling as he sat cross-legged
at a table on the floor, beaded pillows framing his back.
We drove home listening to hair bands on the radio,
naming the guitarists — he's got the blues guys but
I always beat him in hard rock.
As I watched out the window, surrounded by the steady
turn of tires, my head against the headrest,
I would try to catch the poplars
on the roadside — to see them clearly
before they blurred back into
the streaky watercolor landscape.
I had to focus, block out everything else
and stare at the tree — pick a leaf and watch around it,
but only for a moment.
And when I lost it, the car seemed faster, the ground
whirring by.
When we got home, it was my mother who told us,
her usually booming voice a small quiet thing,
completely calm.

## The Fight

We fight like mimes, the dishes or door
or the dog bearing our brunt.
You are showing me that you too
can get things done without being told.
So be it. Done things shine.
Wordlessness is easy. I grew up here.
Only speak when you are the jester, only
seek an audience to entertain. So in silence,
I return to the old me, the new kid,
the small one, only child latchkey.
At home, you are mending the fence
that boxes our garden, fixing the gate.
In the woods, I am walking, listening
to birds and their gossip, moving
so easily farther and farther in.

## August Prep

Four crates of tomatoes
grace the late August kitchen.

My muscles still jump from
hauling them when I find

Rob has died of cancer,
his young wife and two kids

sending messages they've had
years to rehearse.

In the massive saucepot, we've gathered
lids, bands, funnel, rack

flats of jars create a glass layer
in the trunk of the car and

we are carrying them slowly
into Annette's kitchen

and for a moment, the air
smells of deathand tomatoes.

But the pot of water is already boiling
on the stove, and next to it

a bowl of ice and water and the perfect
paring knives we picked

when we did this last year,
and we all begin — hot, then cold,

then peel back the skin and core.
It's the only way to get it all done.

*House* by Justin Hamm

Joel Lipman

## Gulls Along The Lakeshore

At the County Historical Society
a wall of rusty photographs
and sepia tones, magenta
bleeding the faded edges,
long lines of foot soldiers,
so-called *cannon fodder,*
raise rifles and charge
into the lead rain of battle.

From the museum's window,
I gaze across a panorama
of lakeshore sand
and slate blue sky,
as the flock of white bellied gulls
and gray backed terns
spread their wings
as one and lift.

## The Rocks

Red granite bulwarks
and grainy schist hulks
block Kenosha's shore
from storms' erosive surge
and riptide boil.

Like a scarab I scramble across
quarried rock, breakwater stone,
pink veins of quartz, pyrite glint,
calcic clams, mica flakes, silica
shuddering in the lake's
deep rheum and roil.

Over undulating Michigan's
water and sky horizon, I stare
east into the arc's apogee
of dawn above the planet's orb
toward unseen Muskegon,

drop low and into darksplashed,
crannied drafts under pilings
and groaning boulders
while water fills and ebbs
and undertow's purge and pull
tempts my foot's grip
or grasping hand's intent
with each wave's pulse and lapse.

Then, in a drillbit bore, I hide
a treasure of beach gems and bones,
and like a sand crab lad, dart
from the musky caves
and wave-splashed slabs
into melting dusk and bed
with afterlight's long blue duet
of foghorn toll and bell buoy gong.

# Hairy Vegetables

You won't find hairy vegetables at the co-op anymore.
They were eaten by the poor, who sat for hours waiting
with their wretched children, brats without drawers.
The death of hairy tomatoes and hairy peppers, hairy stalks
of celery, hairy eggplants and hairy capers makes
  senseless poetry,
a gyroscope of suffering, spinning science, scales like eczema.
Before the Garden, Chapter One of the timeless serial,
everything was new, nothing plowed nor conquered —
  air, stars, forests, wonders
of darkness, all land precious and holy. Still no dollars.

Surprising, a few years later the calendar, parking lots,
  grid lock, houses on top of houses on top of houses,
  county drain commissioners.
What rivers endure in the name of flood control,
  urban planning —
stuff gets called *a miracle,* but it's not, it's labor, slaughter.
And before I forget about hairy vegetables, there was a time
before antiques and mini marts, when all was hairy —
hairy fish, hairy fowl, hairy insects, God's great beard,
  Willie Nelson.
Jungle cities, hairy temples. Then the bead, shekel, guinea,
  dinar, peso.
Religious order. Slavery. Torture by fire, water.
The New World was sheer horror.

No war is a good war, I don't care how you prove and argue —
I've seen enough flags to gift wrap China. Everybody's
  cemetery full of sad flags, flapping cannon cloth,
  a silent chorus.
Agribusiness artichokes, no-name meat, Jenny Craig,
  Consumer Reports,
highways of Velveeta Cheese spread city to city, hundreds of
theme parks, thousands of supermarkets. Don't get nostalgic —
our sentences exist in the aisles of FoodTown, tracks stop
at Jewel, doors slide wide at Trader Joe's, data
shows you less likely to die violently cashing out at Safeway
than in your living room reading poetry.

The price for it: populations gone bloohey, global fruit,
  drone drops,
fish farms replacing seas, ethanol wheat, drought and heat.
Extinct animal nests in computer chips, digital tics,
gene maps, top dog politics, no hairy vegetables.

Dianne Borsenik

## Train, Loud, Lonesome, Leaving Without Me

Concrete never kept me,
fences never held me back.

Wings are for wind,
hands for folding sunshine,

mouths for holding hearts.
The tattoo of wheels on tracks

clatters loud and lonesome
in someone else's story.

Me? I'll barefoot the rails
after they've cooled,

a balancing act of foolhardiness
and faith, caution left hanging

in the long morning, distant
whistle moonlighting as map.

## Good Time

*Monday, April 18*
*leaving Missouri, north on I35*
*through Iowa*

he says
first time
I've had it up

to a hundred
might as well
keep it up

might as well make
good time
while we can

## Church of the Mind

*–Sunday, August 21, 2017*

One more climb up the too-steep stairs to the apartment, one final look around. Austere walls enclave the ghosts of holidays, passionate celebrations both cheerful and tearful. A tumble of flashes—get-togethers spanning four years' time—but nowhere to sit and remember. The refrigerator shelves are bare of food and drink; the cupboards over the sink are the next to be packed. The bathroom is spotless; it would be sacrilegious to flush the toilet and make sound in this holy place.

all these boxes
stuffed full of
empty rooms

*Church* by Justin Hamm

Steve Henn

## Fresh Fried Chicken for Lunch

In 5th grade, one boy's mother
brought him KFC at lunchtime.
Brought it straight into the classroom.
He'd wheedle and whine
thank you mommy I love you.
He looked like Chunk from Goonies
so we called him Sloth. He tried hard
to be friendly so we hated him.

Joking about Weight Watchers
about donut dinners followed with
mashed potatoes for dessert.
I learned from my own mother
a lack of self control was something
shameful. It was like, to make us
look at that behavior was so rude.

Eventually a boy who played Army
earnestly kicked him in the head
on the playground after lunchtime
while he cowered and whimpered
and whimpered and begged.
I remember the shameful feeling then.
Some of us felt we'd gone too far.
Some of us felt he'd earned it.

# PostPunk LoveSong in the Key of Banal Loathing

Why are we always asked
to consider the restorative properties
of Himalayan Salt? I'd like to see success
fully marketed worldwide mass
suicide. Get in on *The Big Die Off.*
Sponsored by Kool-Aid. If your
coffeehouse pitch highlights your variety
of flavored syrups already I'm skeptical.
Yes I am that hipster. I'm fat.
You wanna fight? Let's fight. Let's fight
because I'm fat. I could sit on you.
I could force feed you serenity and
make a foie gras of your self-satisfied liver.
You might show me yo
yo tricks. Et cetera until we're 21st Century
Jack and Neal joyriding cross country
as if we've never been abominably
sad while scrolling internet dating sites
at 1:30 a.m. with phones that mind
fuck our circadian rhythms.
I'm ready, finally, to be told what to do.
I've never better been prepared for masochism.

## Center Stage

I'll just be center stage congratulating myself
until I vomit up my gall bladder and a ball peen hammer.

I'll just be crapping on the hood of your Lincoln Towncar.

I'll just be rambling incoherently about my Jesus who is
the best Jesus who is the only Jesus who is the true
Jesus and how stupid you are because stupidly, you are.

I'll just be howling.

I'll just be sitting behind home plate
flossing my bloody teeth.

I'll just be twitching and gripping a fake hip
swinging it straight at your noggin
now show me the stars.

I'm sour and full of vinegar like a psychotic pickle.

This world is giving me the heebie fucking jeebies
I would like to relax my grip.

Margaret Crocker

## Two In The Smoking Section

The fly lights on broken dishes,
only he is gentle here.
The food a wave's crust,
the garbage spears,
the shattered ashes,
the rusted clumps of scum,
all are caressed by his wing.
The molded holes of fruit pits,
the running meat,
the ruined young of birds,
the rotting papers,
all are solid by his feathered arm
and by mine.

I watch
and gather his crushed brethren around me,
crying,
for now they do not help he and I
to consume this buffet
of error and fickle use.

# Holy Day

Sunday
is not a Sunday
on Tuesday
no matter what the state says,
and I will not suffer a Tuesday to live
in pancakes
or rainy mornings
or dogs gone patient and sleepy
at the foot of the bed.

Sunday
could never be an appointment with the eye doctor,
or bills or waiting,
shift differential,
a working lunch,
nirvana or real redemption
with a long, hard board at my back
and the holy mother
suffering for my eyes.

Sunday will never work
no matter what Teamsters say so,
will never clean,
will never rise at dawn,
will never dismiss the cloudless day
or the smells of syrup and coffee.

It will not begrudge me
the desultory hair of the dog at 10,
the abandonment of lawn implements by 12,
the sweatpants at 2,
the sandwiches for dinner,
the book,
opened and forgotten for Tuesday,
and your face.
It would never touch your face,
swathed in blankets
and haloed by some slant of the drapes
that makes time
and me
love you on Sunday.

## The Days Of My Death

*No one escapes life alive.*

-African proverb

*What the fuck?*

-some guy, dying

Today is the day I will die.

In the dark,
there is only the alarm,
while my feet find themselves to lead me through the gauntlet,
black ceiling,
static,
sleeping fur at my toes,
sharp edges,
a blurry light in the field of my vision,
feet slide,
fingers shuffle,
searching, feeling, bumping, frantic
to stop the noise.
Stop the noise.

I am awake.

There are screens then,
to show me pretty pictures,
to label things correct, alarming or Def-con 4,
and I thank sweet Jesus for coffee machines with timers.

Internal lists begin to re-establish their hold,
I turn on my phone
I pull on my clothes
and I begin, again,
to enter the land of the living
and show,
with good grooming,
how civilized I can be.

Work is work.
I don't push a barrow,
I don't harvest this winter's pantry,
I don't kill or cure,
I don't stretch hides.
I fill eight hours to receive weekly paper that may or may not be vaguely related to the gold standard,
the Illuminati or Ancient Aliens,
whichever,
papers that I curse and wait for like Christmas,
papers that I shove around to different places with increasingly complex calculations,
papers that are dead, dead, dead,
and not even edible anymore.

It is evening.
The children are gone,
my man is gone,
and only the cats remain.

My god,
where did we get so many cats?
Everyone knows they steal your breath,
they're unlucky,
they like the number 13,
they're born with a middle paw straight to the heavens
and two feet in the grave
and they're watching.
They're always watching to see what we will give.
I have nothing.
I gave at the office,
feet and fingers and brain.

The evening is a beer,
warm water
and more moving pictures to oblivion.
And then, tomorrow.

Tomorrow is the day I will die.

*Sublimis labes* by Jim McGowin

Daniel Crocker

## Hulk Meets Moloch

and can do nothing but stare in wonder
at the magnificent power of something
so malevolent

Betty wants to buy a house
in the suburbs

Bruce doesn't care as long
as it's close to his lab

But Hulk wants a simpler life
Something away from the American
flags and Trump signs

but he's so big what apartment
would fit him
What god of mercy
would allow him this

He knows his mind isn't right

There are no jobs for him
None that he would take anyway
Split personality, you say?

Hulk never corrects them.
Why don't you go back to smashing?
You're good at it.

Hulk gets so tired of smashing
and with Betty's help
he's been working on his pronunciation

He doesn't want to be this anymore
He doesn't want to smash brains
across concrete and aluminum

Still he knows his mind isn't right
and neither is Banner's
and sometimes he even worries
about Betty with her father
bent on death

With the tanks and guns
With the military complex
A burning  hatred of Hulk
Hulks wonders if he's America
or if he's the things America hates
Bisexual, mentally ill, so used to night
he feels swaddled in a blanket of darkness

In some ways, though, he
knows he's better off than Bruce
who has to worry about the long term
when Hulk doesn't
Bruce wonders what will happen
if he has to go back into the hospital
check himself in through the ER

Suicidal, homicidal, delusional

Nervous, Bruce gets so goddamned
nervous.

# Bruce Banner's Intrusive Thoughts

For this poem we have to pretend
that Bruce Banner has a daughter
and that Bruce Banner isn't me

We'll have to pretend that the basement
I write in is his lab

Okay?

Bruce had a fight with Betty
Bruce's anxiety was out of control
Bruce's OCD was even worse
Bruce's OCD manifests itself
as intrusive thoughts
he can't help but articulate out loud
Bruce is about to have his dog put down
just like me
Bruce's dog is going to die
just like mine

Bruce paces the lab
He says, I'm
going to die today
Bruce says it several times
His daughter overhears

She calls Betty
Dad is saying scary things
I think you should come home

Dad is saying scary things
Dad is having scary thoughts
Betty, who we must pretend isn't
my wife
tells her daughter it's nothing to worry
about. It's his anxiety

No one knows if it's something to
worry about or not. But it's what
we tell ourselves. It's what we tell
our daughter.

## Hulk Gets Philosophical

Of all the people Hulk
could have been with
he ended up with a
man so frail he can
barely live with the thought

that there is anger built
into him. That he is
dangerous

A man who Sexton
might have said is
waiting to die

Is that true, Bruce
Bruce, is that true

Bruce doesn't answer

He never answers.

Shawn Pavey

## Breakfast with Baldinger

*As your lawyer,* he starts,
*I recommend that you take the day*
*off from work. Start with edible marijuana*
*to take care of that hangover in spectacular fashion*
*and coat it all with French toast. Play guitar for a while,*
*then spend the afternoon at the art museum.*
*Follow that with a spicy Bloody Mary and barbecue*
*for a late lunch. Swing by Prospero's to shoot the shit with Tom.*
*Resist buying the beat up hardcover 10 volume collection*
*of the World's Greatest Poetry.*
*Retire to home to drink gin bucks*
*and watch Otis Rush play an Epiphone Casino*
*upside down and left handed on DVD*
*in Dolby Surround Sound.*

## Stunted Spring

Let a cold mist fall
on an early spring day
glazing a light covering of snow.
Quiet, except for a Kansas wind
battering trees in the backyard.
Listen and hear the winter's dead
limbs crack and crash into the hard earth
still rigid with cold and you will know
you are still in Kansas
and that winter is not done with you.
No, not with you.

## Robert Johnson at the Crossroads

You've got to spin the bottle just so.
Put the right amount of hip check
and pool cue English on it.
Needs to be a night like this
where lightning just looks
for something to strike
and there's blood, of course,
from a knife cut deep
in the left palm meat.

Then, well man, then
you just have to wait.

Think long and hard
on that thing you can't
live without anymore. For me,
it's this '28 Gibson. I swear
to God that some nights
she'll sing sweeter than
any bird you ever heard
but not every night, you know?
Not every night.

An old man with a shiny cane
takes the bottle with my blood
and drinks every goddamn drop,
licks his lips, and pulls some papers
out of his dark jacket pocket.

*You don't need to read that, son.*
*Just dip this pen into that cut.*
*You want to make your mark, now,*
*don't you?*

*Won't cost you anything you're using, anyway.*

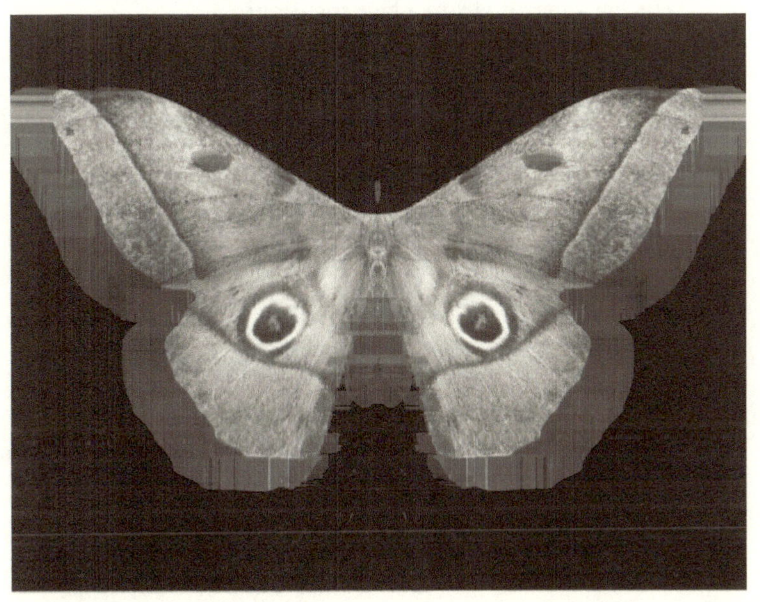

*Motabilis oculus* by Jim McGowin

Jeanette Powers

## Bites: essays from the Gasconade

Are you suffering from a face mauling?
Covered in 10,000 micro-ticks?

Then join me n Puppy Mas in the valerian root and wine-inspired thought-coma we've both entered. We are covered in oil and freshly bathed with bug-sprayed bed and new sheets and let me ask you to try to stop looking for ticks once you've found even one.

Welcome to the dark side of being outside. I am heartily convinced that this minor insectoid setback won't deter me from finding a place to build my aerie, but I'm beginning to think trees may be less than perfect. Puppy and I started our search today at just after dawn with this gentle dawn.

That's Lily's pasture and just north of it, at the 11 o'clock of this imaginary photo is the cow pasture. By the way, those strings that seem to keep the cows back, they're electrified. Good to know. We head past the lazily curious beef-to-be's back to our back path from yesterday. This path is magnificent. Wandering, also lazy, clear walking. I found a bunch of these weird mushrooms. Saw these sticks broken beautifully, too. There's lots of ways you can tell a path is well trod, and lots of broken sticks is one of them.

These tiny dark purple flowers with nearly black leaves are everywhere. There are fewer small dry creek beds as on the other side of the road. You can see that the water runoff mainly uses this path to go downhill. The path is flat on one side and a foot-deep ravine on the other. I'm remembering we're still in the cow pasture, it's big.

The path feeds out into a meadow with all sorts of directions to head in. I count three to start with, one to each side, smaller maybe for deer. The third is the obvious choice because it's the easy crossing for a nice looking, new creek: flowing. That's the way I'm gonna go but just want to skirt the rest of the meadow. There's a sittin' tree, for sure.

Sittin' Trees are tall trees that have fallen over, but kept on living. Their trunk lays on the ground strong instead of rotten, a place you walk to to get away. Puppy investigates a big lump of white on the ground, so I head over there. Someone has left their mark here, suddenly I'm a professional archaeologist! I've found some sort of white marblish sculpture-thing which is without a doubt man-made. What stories will it tell of the people who came before!? I like this angle for a photograph because it will look like the statue is taking a selfie.

I keep walking. I see it before Puppy does, our first skeleton, now I'm like a NatGeo level professional archaeologist! Bones, definitely a femur, ribs, jawbone and further on, a skull. This appears to be a 21st century member of the Bovine Blahteblah Species probably died in a flash flood from the nearby creek and fed mountains of families of animals which fed planets of micro-ticks which now feast on me. The vertebrae are my favorite bones. To *have a spine* is much better then *lend a hand* or *knee-jerk reaction.*

I wander over to the creek and luckily am quietly gazing along the right-hand side of the creek bed when there's a deer, bout the width of your grandparent's house away. She leaps high enough to scale pop-pop's garage door. It's fucking majestic, but that's absolutely not what I'm thinking at all. *Fucking Puppy.* Without question, there is no question, that none other than puppy flushed that deer and he's about to be off for miles. This is the dreaded deer chase, feared by every dog's slave (*erhrm, owner*) and the content of so many hushed campfire tales of loss.

The deer is at the top of its graceful leap, it's been exactly .2 of a second. I scream: *OLLY MAS! ABSOLUTELY NOT! HEP! HEP! HEP!*

Full name out, the inexplicable knee-jerk scream of *absolutely not*, the mega-command-function, the distance correction: HEP! I don't have the first idea where that sound came from, probably my Grandfather, but it works. Yelling (or dog, probably both) flushes 7 more deer of all sizes and antlers and tan coat and a grace under pressure I am not even close to exhibiting. I just keep yellin for the dog to not obey his doggy nature. Basically for no other reason than I don't want to have to worry about him for the next two hours.

At this moment, Murph (the yellow lab with the limp and the stick and the panting) shows up. Wow, where the fuck am I?

I holler for Puppy Mas another minute or so when he comes trotting back from his dance with the deer. Now the pack of us head to the crossing. My first email address on the internet was "yellowleaf." I always found a particular beauty in the changing of color and falling though the sky. It's not terribly surprising that over 20 years of looking within that *radical change* and *flying blind* are my top metaphors. They are everywhere I am.

We're back at the river house where the kayaks stay. Amazing. What a less strenuous path than the main road. We stop by the river and head up to watch the river from the broad expanse of decks. And that's when the tick horrorshow began. I look down at my arm and it is visibly crawling with nearly invisible tiny parasites. Oh, *jesus-pete,* that means they are all over the dog, too.

I sit nicely in the sun where I can see better and pull a dozen micro-ticks head and all out of my knee skin. Then arm. Then … Fuck. They. Are. Everywhere.

Mike James

## Traveler's Fable

A hotel, sick of ins and outs and noise complaints and made up stories at the hotel bar. Yes, a hotel sick of laundered sheets and room service and little scented soap bars and muffled one night stands. This hotel dreamed itself into a lunchbox, carried by a man at the mill. Opened and shut only a few times each day. There only for him. A thermos, the best company. The thermos once a lighthouse, years before.

## Folk Tale Without Neon Or Blessings

*for Shawn Pavey*

God was tired, so she took the day off. She was sick of panic and endless needs. Sick of that old scale of wants versus thanks. Couldn't fathom another roundabout day of angels gossiping over people whose magic scars they guessed at.

So, after yoga and a garden walk, she carved for hours on a rock she couldn't lift and studiously didn't think of kids. Late in the day, in dust white work clothes, with wind blowing just enough to lighten green on grass and leaves, she sat and sipped her tea and wondered how anything she ever made could still exist.

## On Love Affairs, Break Ups, & Such

Heart plus flowers equals a drug store valentine. Open the card. There's a door inside. Behind the door, a tunnel goes down farther than light shows. Don't be afraid of the dark. Tell yourself that again and again, like an old man in an ancient church saying thankless prayers. Go on in. Delight in the cold. Your hunger comes in waves, directed by the moon. It ebbs and flows.

*Imperialis mutata* by Jim McGowin

## John Burroughs

### Unfounded

In this city of lost places
my fifteen-year-old granddaughter
is no longer hiding
all the places she cuts
herself to hide
all the places
she hurts.

I imagine it's because she does not
want to die
and the cutting makes her
feel alive
or because she feels
dead inside
or like—            hell
I can only speculate why
because she cannot
tell.

In my city of lost places
there are six urns—
two wooden boxes
a metal canister
and three fancier ones
from the funeral home—

full of ashes and bone bits
our dogs Lucky and Lady
her eighteen-year-old cat Cricket
my mother-in-law
sister-in-law Sheree
and wife Geri Lynne
because I cannot bear
to bury them.

in my city of lost places
there is a light that never goes out
and there is an out that never gets lit
and there is a fit that never gets fought
and there is an it that never gets
sought or wrought

In my city of lost places
the oyster is my world
until it is not anymore
and still is and there is
a this that cannot be that
and there is an at
that cannot be bliss
and it seems all things
are hurting and healing
and feeling like cutting themselves.

In my city of lost places
a seamstress has come undone
a teacher has failed to master the lesson
and a doctor has caught his death.

I imagine it's because she does not
want to live
and the cutting makes her
feel dead
or loved inside
or like—            hell
I can only speculate
and expectorate why
when I do
not know.

In my city of lost places
it's the first anniversary
of my wife's death
her clothing is still in our dresser
and hanging in my closet
and the black framed family
photo collage from her
hospital room still
sits in my living room
on her former make-up table
and her make-up is still
in my bathroom with her tweezers
and scissors and razor

and whatever has not yet been cut
is torn apart
and I feel her
with me and not
and realize sometimes it's easier
to love your mate unconditionally
when she no longer expects
anything of you.

## No Other

*after Far Enemy by Tony Ingrisano*

A wide web of geometry and pixilation
looms over my brick suburban bungalow.

The colors warm and entice me
with creeping florescent sophistication.

I feel them drawing me up and in
while equally I am drawing them inside.

It's a network of jasmine attraction
bringing untoward craving and resentment,

hate and cruelty from America the beautiful,
Russian bots, unacknowledged racists,

television networks, Amazon.com, nihilism
proponents, penile enhancement specialists,

trolls, moles, sexist pols and ad-mongers,
while the colors of it all bleed into pools

of need and reaction, stupefaction,
failure to listen disguised as debate,

hasty action, dystopian dissatisfaction,
snark disguised as lark and warring factions.

This poem began as an expression of appreciation
for a wide web of precious colors and pixilation

before I met the so-called far enemies
in my bathroom mirror and hardly

recognized them as something other
than other.

## Ataraxis

*after Equanimity by Dana Oldfather*

incline into
equanimity
earth blood
green mud
recline into
infinity
be bud
be home
be om
namo bhagavate vasudevaya
insh'allah wah
there is no
there is know sew
be bloom
be lilt
be boom
be wilt
heal merry
full of grays
judge nothing
black or white
more or less
all calm
nam myoho renge kyo

hello good why
sway marigold
do chai tea
sip t'ai chi
I knead know
need no dough
no mantra
am not I
we are eye
are know
need no labels
seek not
need not find
untangle ataraxis
un-angle collapse
not without feeling
flowing into serenity
simple complexity
complex simplicity
simply see
and be
equanimity

Kevin W. Peery

## Chokecherry Tree

The
same
night
lightning
struck
our
chokecherry
tree...
the
neighbors
said
they
could
see
a
fireball
flash...
just
moments
before
the
twister
hit
and
all
hell
broke
loose.

## Eagle Lane

After a
poetry reading
at Barb's Books
in Belle...
we made
our way
back
to the
rural studio
off Eagle Lane...

Our plan
was to
fire up
some brats...
before
a late
evenin' storm
set in...

Pavey had
a new
Chicago blue
Les Paul
to show me...

and I
remember sayin'
that if
I wasn't
such a hack...
I'd certainly
like to
plug it in
for a
test drive...

As
lightnin' flashes
filled their
great room...
Edmonson's
latest work
triggered
the most genuine
asthetic response
I've experienced
in over
a decade...

When the
brats and
baked potatoes
were ready
we sat down

at an antique
farm table...
passin' around
condiments
like a joint
at a Tom Petty
concert...

And midway
through this
magnificent meal...
Edmonson
kindly remembered
some Wasabi Sauce
that made
my palate do
the old
soft shoe...

Dorsey
held court
after supper...
and we
spoke at length
about
California Bloodlines...
Americana songwriters
and documentary
film making...

We shared
Banquet beer...
small batch bourbon
and some
of the
best
war stories
I've heard
in a
long
long
time

## Six Pack To Go

I
still
get
a
funny
feelin'
when
we
roll
through
Skidmore...

Ya
see
I
was
only
seven....
when
they
gunned
his
big
ass
down...

He
was
just
sittin'
in
his
Chevy...
outside
the
D&G
Tavern...

A
blood
spattered
six
pack
to
go

in
the
floorboard...
and
freshly
lit
Salem...
still
smolderin'
between
his
lips

*Diner* by Virginia Harold

Stefene Russell

## Four Little Histories

1.

In the train station photo booth,
a quarter dropper waits.

He escaped the backyard
where his Tesla coil hums
and makes the dogs bark.
Blue electricity
tinsels his hair.

He shivers in his brown plaid overcoat,
the one with the frayed collar.
His pockets: full of metal shavings.
His head: uncovered.

His winter hat, the one lined
with squirrel, rests upside down
in his lap, under trembling
hands, the fur standing on end.

2.

A middle-aged lady
in blue smock (appears
gray in photo).

It's her third stop today
at the Mold-o-Rama kiosk.

In her hand, a new, warm
animal. Lumpy and
ferocious.The wax still soft.
Its face a thumbprint.

She brandishes it at the camera
like it's an Oscar.

3.

The bicycle-eater,
ran away from the midway.

He broke his contract
with the barker. He poses
in front of painted palm trees
because he has fifty cents
and a face.

He bares his teeth
then takes a bite
from the rubber bulb
of a bicycle horn.

Chews with his mouth open
with the delight of a kid
who just popped a balloon.
He chews those rubber fragments
just to hear them squeak.

4.

She has the kind of face you wouldn't
remember without a picture. Which is why
she's taking a picture.

She's holding up a Number Rose:
four hearts and four crowns of pollen.
One bloom smells like four.

First was the soldier. Then, the baker.
The butcher. An accountant. Never,
for some reason, the candlestick maker.
So in her other hand: a candelabra.

This is the way she looks as she
remembers a rare miniature rose
called *Why Not.*

Melvin Litton

## Hard West

Scarred by Dakota winds and dead-end roads,
where hundred-car freights of loaded coal pass
ghost farms, graves, and pasture bones,
where a redhead mourns her road-killed man
in midnight bars with one-night stands,
and an old hombre rides alone at
night in answer to el coyote's cry,
where the blues still hatch them old
refrains of murder, lust, and winter rains …
Beneath the dust lays ocean rock
and above the land an endless sky,
where shadows labor to the sun
in thirst for water, oil, and love till
even a damn fool's gotta know
he's been fishin' in the wrong hole …
But hit town at sundown, cast regret away
on whiskey, bets, and naked sweat in chance
for a better day … as night deepens, cars wreck,
lives too in haste and ruin…with bare hands
you grip the wheel on a rutted road to
the distant hills where all is given and all
is blest, face another sunrise in the Hard West …

# Unearthed

Older than the sharks, down tooth river
we'd crawl through its sand and clay beds
where the sleeping fossils lived when Kansas
was a sea, before the waters placed the shadows
of their flesh upon the cliffs to draw the child's hand
in question of unanswered time, where the secret nibbles
at the riddle and the soft underbelly of clouds harden
into armor-plated storms of assaulting night
like a murderer yet unjudged, unborn …

## Off Work

Driving home, passed a rusted-out
Mustang, its tailpipe dangling like a
donkey's dick tasting the breeze ...
Hell, made me laugh, week's end,
I too rolled down my window to lap
the wind, felt like an Egyptian mummy
just unwrapped from a 40-century sleep,
flesh sore and mind numb, awakened like
Frankenstein in want of woman, beer,
and music to light my soul again ...

*Eat the Rich* by Virginia Harold

Lori Brack

## The curator of flower demise

lights little wax votives for petals,
sepals, secret deep tongues
where lily's manufacture seeps.
She keeps bottles and jars
with screw tops and stoppers,
glass sequesters of tomato blossom
equally white and deep green,
lilac's heavy lavender, something red
that reminds her of the French aunts.
Jasmine says one paper label.
Vervain replies another. A going
toward the wet garden, a gate.

## At the Snow Museum

Walkers sidestep the revolving door once they catch a whiff of what's inside. Constant winter blusters behind glass, blowing flakes the size of a baby's palm or small and sharp as shards of sky. You remember. Yellow light blurs the icy kitchen window and red boots squeak as you follow her down the middle of the slippery street. It is later than you've ever been. Or earlier. In the street-light, snow swarms like summer moths. White tracks fill up behind you.

## At the Museum of Lost Things

When she cracks open a window in this edifice without
doors, a jumble of the missing waits. Uncatalogued,
no labels reveal the dates. Each time she looks in, she sees
another thing, as if hands rearranged, acquired and culled
the collection, toiled in darkness. A doll lamp her mother
dressed in rosy fabric. Bright taste of clove. A specific green
dish photographed with snow and purple afternoon
blooming of the mirabilis flower. One slick gray booklet
called *Our Lady of Fatima* that came in the mail addressed
only to her.

Roy Beckemeyer

## Angels Fallen From Clouds

Angels lost to the sky
    become angular,        wooden,
wings sawn      from rough blocks
    of cedar,      pinions       no      more
      than ruinous marks      of gouges      slashed
   haphazardly,              shoved into
      slabs        unevenly,          splintered
  at edges,      in only   gross contiguity
       to frayed      feathers,     all      too
dense, too        substantial
  to      flog        flight
     from    clouds.

## Remembering Louis Armstrong At Perdition

What better way to sound
the end of the world? *The*
*Armageddon Brass.* Seven
trumpets. One for each
note of the scale. They
play in order, east to
west, descending thereby
into cacophony, the rules
of harmony fractured,
their horns lengthening,
evolving like living beings,
bending notes to screeches,
screams. Seventh Trumpet turns
to the Conductor, mouths
the word *Now?* Nods,
purses his lips, presses them
into the mouthpiece, pulls
the other six into a unison blast,
right on key, the 4-bar rapture of
of Louis Armstrong's *West End Blues*
trumpet solo—the sustained glory
of that final high B.

## Forward Angel Control

The Oracle Angel, banner
in hand, looks down
on the burden of Babylon.

*Red Death, this is Big Boy.*
*Fire Mission. Grid 755463,*
*Direction six-six-zeero-zeero.*
*Fire for effect.*

*Whoa, Black Angel,*
*adjust fire. Range*
*short, deviation left.*

*Lightning Archangel!*
*Emergency target.*
*Immediate fire.*

*Death's Doorstep,*
*Six plus three zero. Hack!*
*Bring on the weapons*
*of His indignation.*

*Their faces shall be as flames,*
*boys, their faces shall be as flames.*

*Parlor* by Virginia Harold

Benji Kuzemka

I only trust a god who remembers
that I need more than mere salvation,

which like all things
is magnified
by a story, a good clove of garlic,
a magnificent slap on the ass.

My epochs are the most real
and impermanent of things.

I can convince neither
you nor me
of utter unabstraction.

But do let November come.

She was a real rubster
of the Olive Garden variety—

the stuff plain Hershey bars
are made of.

I imagine her still happy
and hating my back hair.

I study all the fruit futures,
the pierced bellies.

Am I still a gracious host?
Have I forgotten the feel
of a coffee grinder come midnight?

No amount of this now-warm belgian blonde
can erase the fact that God once told Zephaniah
that    war rape was cool.

That means that he watched the Eastern front and Nanking
with a bowl of buttered celestial popcorn
not even watching the commercials flashing between our
precious little wars
and hemorrhaging genitalia.

One of those singing reality shows was on channel four
and its well known that he never misses an episode.

## Jason Vaughn and W.E. Leathem

# …of a feather

### I. *Midpoint*

*After three years away from Kansas, I am sitting in my old merciful green chair in the living room of a temporary "home" in a sleepy neighborhood in Basehor, an orange dog asnore at my feet. This is where my parents are staying until their next house (the house) is arranged on the sweep of pastureland they purchased before I drove back. I am staying with them only until I get a job or come up with a life-plan that might lead me to another state or country or universe. The house is cramped, my room stuffed with unpacked boxes waiting to be moved again. This living room, despite the dog bed that Buddy hardly ever lies on, offers the safest path. And now, needing to stretch my legs once more, I step over our charmingly-smelly buddy and pad across the brown shag carpet. Parting the course whitish curtains on the wide front window, I look out into the afternoon. A mere dusting of winter has prettified the ugliest metals and plastics and surfaces of car, mailbox, pavement. Such icing-sugar views are just one of the possibilities I missed when I lived and wrote screenplays amid the stifling streety bustle of Los Angeles, where people seem to live for the sun and the scrub-drab hiking hills and the blank blue skies and the rains falling so rarely that, when they do fall, the joy-shock of the sound makes you feel as if that's the reason you stayed. So, I have come (returned) to the center of the country. My country. Yet I'm feeling as aimless as ever in a story that has no ending. There's a fear in this, but also the rosy idea that anything can happen. The kicker—and maybe it's a gift—is that none of us can plan a single DAMN thing.*

## II. My Gear

I toss my gear on the bed: a satchel with my laptop, a bag with my portable Bose speakers, a pair of sweats, a toothbrush, a half-pint Amsterdam bottle repurposed and now containing Listerine. All humphed half a mile down through the cold from the car parked by the chicken coup at the top of the hill.

There is comfort recognizing that deep winter has exiled my semi-irrational fear of spiders and other crawly things. What is it, anyway, about shared facilities that seems to invite tiny livestock to congregate in showers, dawdle in drawers or take up residence between sheets? In the kitchen, clean dishes stand in the drying rack. Glasses settle on a folded paper towel. I slide items picked up at the market in town into the fridge: a bottle of decent red wine, some garlic-stuffed olives, a round of brie. A box of veggie crackers goes on top of the microwave. I keep the half pint of Evan Williams in my pocket.

The Baron, once again home following a six-week sabbatical, already has his computer open, a phone to his ear. Coltrane plays from its tinny speakers. Vaughn, down to check things out ahead of next month's residency, has dropped his stuff by the door and now paces out on the deck.

I pull a hoodie over three layers. Over this, my green jacket. Not really substantial enough for the dropping mercury, it is sufficient to turn the wind, leave the layers to do their thing. I add a stocking cap and a pair of yellow workman's gloves. It'll do.

It's been a good six months since I was last out to Belle. It was warm then, warm enough for Jeanette, the Baron and I to drag the chairs from under the sycamore and out into the river to sit chest deep in the flow, to spend an afternoon talking about Dorsey's new book, to crack a beer and let the water carry away the heat and city dust. Saw a couple of the boys up in the city, since: A book release. Jason, aka the Baron, passing through *en route* home for the holidays.

Vaughn adjusts his hat and gloves. He's added one of those puffy synthetic vests. We strike off, paralleling the anemic, westering sun. Trailing the Gasconade's flow. *I, who've never done a stint at OAC, as tour guide.*

We tramp the shore's tree line. Ambling at us from all corners of the property, half a dozen dogs. They fall in line behind. I'm surprised to see Murph. Figured winter would be it for him, but here he is, happy, lumbering along on his bad hips. Present and accounted for: Zeus and Aphrodite, their muzzles greying. Miley, the sweetest pussy cat of all Rottweilers, reconnoiters a brief, *hey-what's-going-on-here* before trundling off to see to her own business. There's a frisky black dog I don't recall. And the newest addition to the pack, a silver and black rottie pup that galumphs along nipping at my pant leg.

What is it about farm dogs that's so qualitatively different from city dogs? Are we put off by their diurnal gifts of gnawed deer legs and half-eaten armadillos? Do we love them any less because we do not let them inside the house? Do the hunting and killing sounds that haunt the night set us on edge? Do we begrudge them their wildness, staved off as they jostle at the feed bowls? Do we mourn their passing any less due to the unspoken, yet shared, understanding that there will be NO $1,000 vet bills paid?

I don't think so. They, in turn, do not begrudge us these standards so different from those we offer their citified cousins. Farm dogs know that they are free. Free from leashes, free from the indignity of kennels and the humiliating absurdity of dog parks and poop scooped up in grocery baggies.

Vaughn and I pause to smell the river. The far shore fallow with fields. To take in the tracks frozen in mud, a seasonal fossil record of all we've missed while indoors.

We put them to our backs and cross the clearing where yard begins to slip into pasture and then feral wood.

The creek bed is stony and all but dry. Choked with leaves and the wash of last fall's flood. We ford, followed by our new pack.

Up in the lower meadow, grass is beat down into clumps. Cow piles refresh the recollection of last season's purpose for this acreage. In the back pasture, the white stones of an old sculpture lie toppled. Edges gone green, now blacken with lichen. Yet, the visible intention of human touch. Too heavy to right, we move on.

We cross an electric fence. In summer, we'd toss a jacket over its top to escape the shock. Today, gloves and layers and winter's thicker fabrics allow for more haphazard passage. The stream pools. The ground is mucky, a sure sign of an earth-fed spring somewhere upland. As the ravine meanders to the north, we hew south. Climb the ridge. Stones slip and skitter away. Under the canopy of the softwood, wind rattles the last of the leaves clinging like holocaust survivors to the branches.

A quarter mile on we stand, winded. Atop the bluff. A small stand of fir conceals an upturned rowboat gone to rot. Through its beam, a tree grows. Here, the wind picks up, canters along the ridgeline. We take advantage of a shed. Empty. We almost miss it. Its stone and chipping paint blend well into the palate of the season. Three walls of glass make greenhouse good on the day's feeble rays. Once warm, we push on.

We cross the field buffering a pasture that, in turn, buffers Eagle Lane. Heads on the half dozen cows that cluster around an old enclosure turn to follow. At the drive, we turn toward the blacktop, postpone the inevitable, if just for a while. A FedEx truck, blundering like a wagon of Keystone Cops, spews dust and forces us into the verge.

At the top of the property: what a view! Yellow and henna land folds and swells. Bisected by empty asphalt, it reaches out toward oncoming dusk. It is getting late. There's nothing for it, so we turn back. On the way, we are again forced off the gravel by the FedEx truck, this time centripetally hurrying along on its outward way.

Back at the river house, we toss our coats over chairs. Switch on the hot pot. The dogs are nowhere to be seen. All is still. Quiet. Lost to my thoughts, I sip hot tea. I stare at the tippy tops of the trees, now peach colored, catching the last of the sun.

Don't feel much like reading at the moment.

Instead, the urge to write. To feel the keys of the laptop soft-shoe beneath my fingers. I suppress an inclination to watch them at their work. Instead, another sip of tea, eyes glued to the horizon as daylight makes its escape…

## III. *The River*

*Before the sun can fully find its way down through the hill trees, I come out of the warm "river house"—after my first night at Osage—to get a breath of icy air and walk the footpath just back of a twiggy bank along the Gasconade, the ground crunching under my feet. An inexorable chocolate-gray current flows thickly by (not fast, not slow, just how it does). If anything, it carries only the sound of my breathing. I wonder if these waters can freeze solid. I wonder how deep they can get. Then my eyes are drawn a little ways to the left of my left foot. In the center of the path a woodpecker lies frozen on its back, shoulders hunched, salt-and-pepper wings held stiffly down the sides of its frame as if it had been standing in attention and then just fell. Its eyelids, delicate as moth material, are shut as intensely as a rousing person's can be when they'd rather stay dreaming. And a bright blush of vermillion, the width of a thumbprint smudge, smears up and over the head, finally finishing down the back of the neck somewhere. Glancing around for anyone who might be watching this watching, the cold air smelling of cold air, every living thing holding still for a moment, I do not whisper to the woodpecker. I almost do. Then I touch the toe of my shoe to the picket of its tail, nudge the body more perpendicular to the river. And go back into the house so that when I return to this place and the bird is gone, it will be because it flew away.*

## IV. Raptors

*Look, there's another...*

They perch in the trees or on road signs, atop barns and silos. Sit along the wires that string from town to town up and down 50 Highway. Maybe it's the slim pickings of the fallow months that bring 'em out. Could be the cleaner sight lines. Could be it's just that white and yellow hawk bellies stand out better against ashen branches and the tawny Wyeth palate of winter fields.

It's a game best played in winter. A game I tend to play as I drive back and forth between the city and the town where my son visits his grandparents.

*Over there!* A finger taps the glass with its middle knuckle, half-thinking. Points out two birds edging a field, wings spread, riding the current of air along the tree line. *Scouting for mice.* Pause. *Could be rabbits, I guess...*

*Too cold for snakes,* notes my fellow road warrior.

A naturalist's game of solitaire. Sometimes I play it with the kids and Leslie. Usually, when just driving lonesome. Something about it reminds me of those essays by Jim Harrison in which there's always food and out-of-doors and the sudden intrusion of a wildlife sighting. Birds, usually.

I stop often to see the ex in-laws. There's always a cup of joe and some catching up. Occasionally, a surprise serving of roasted pigeon or quail - possibly poached earlier that morning at roadside - or some of this year's deer sausage and low fat crackers and that fakey orange cheese from the supermarket. A beer or a shot when late enough. If I'm lucky, there's a meal at *El Espolon* - absolutely the best white-people Mexican food I've had anywhere. Succulent and savory and crispy *Carnitas.* Palate-scorching deep fried chilies. And margaritas that come in two sizes only: 'mondo huge' or 'big as a swimming pool.'

Recently, I've taken to playing as I drive to and from the city and Belle where I drop my friend, *the Baron*, for his stays with the OAC arts colony.

*DANM! and another...*

Yesterday, as we turned off the blacktop at the upper cabins, I spotted a red-headed woodpecker. Set right down on a fallen branch, just idling time. Feathered in a shawl of white and brown speckles. Its head a dollop of flame. Eyeing us with one eye. I startled my companions, leaping from the car even before we'd come to a stop. Darting into the brush, I-phone as camera in hand. It led me a chase. Flitting from tree to tree ever deeper into the wood. Then, with a sideways twist of its head, as if to call out *sucka*! It flew off. I meandered back, unrequited.

My record is twenty-six. That's one hawk every 3.57 miles. Usually, I spy only a dozen or so. Usually, counting only when outward bound from the city.

Today, for whatever reason, I made the decision not to play. To forgo the count. Then, like water settling to its table, I noticed that I was counting.

I numbered four before I mention the game to Vaughn. We are deep into some strand of conversation about the development of character, or the raggle-taggle role of love in modern filmmaking or our distaste for organized sports … organized education … organized religion...

*Did you see that*, I interrupt! *Four on two billboards.*

*A cast of hawks* — that's the word for a group of hawks, did you know that? Two facing one direction, siting tall and rapine like German military insignia. One on the opposite side. Twenty yards along on the very next billboard, a fourth.

Missouri is one of those states that sells its birthright — its pristine vistas — willy-nilly for a pot of cold porridge. In pursuit of every single last drop of profit, every stretch of Missouri highway is trashy with an incessant parade of cheap, tawdry advertisement. Every side of a barn. Every roof of a building that can support infrastructure. Every square mile of roadside green has some sort of sign plastered across it.

Money changers of every stripe hawk insurance, hawk half a dozen different brands of Jesus, hawk gentlemen's clubs and convenience marts and boating equipment and snack food...

Our conversation stretches out like the freeway ahead, unfolds like the miles behind. We both, now, keep eyes peeled. Mile after mile, I scour the passenger side of the road. Vaughn the driver's side. Somewhere along the way, we start counting out loud: *46... 47... 51 ...*

Our final approach to the city is a twisty stretch of highway, a holdover from a time before the four-lane, before not-at-grade crossings. We are in too close. There don't seem to be any more hawks.

As we pass the city limit, I spy one. A magnificent specimen. Regal and alert. Its back to the city, it faces away from the way we are headed.

## V. *Counting Hawks*

*From inside this car flying down US 50, all the hawks look the same. We've counted some. More than enough for a cast. Just not, it seems, a cast of characters. They're hawks. And from this vantage, in this region, they might as well be a single body duplicated into infinity. If I was a hawk (a hawk, with those sharper eyes or simply hawk eyes), each of the winter-fluffed specimens I spied sitting on the droops of wires or the tense shoulders of telephone poles, or plunging suddenly in silent predatory plops to the ochre grass—each of them would likely look as individual as any person looks to another person. The parallels in their shades and postures would not overshadow their distinctive markings or make their bodies, in any possible way, seem hatched out of a mold. And would I wave a wing in hello? Hang my head from the shame of driving instead of soaring? Would I think myself above them? Exalt and join them? Or would I just keep counting hawks until the sun going down made me suddenly as desperate as anyone who'd never counted…*

*Back* by Josh Crow

## Timothy Geiger

### Trash Can Fires

*This was nature.*

—T.C. Boyle's *Greasy Lake*

In the cold dark gathering three teenage boys
watch the fire in a steel drum
summon one orange affirmation of smoke,
a future filled with the faint praise of heat.
Digby, and Jeff, and me, reminisce the recent past—
trips to the boy's room smoking, senior dances
in the parking lot, stolen Pabst Blue Ribbon
and bags and bags of weed.
We don't speak, or believe in any
hoodoo spirits—our desires lurk below our brows,
bangs that cover our eyes—in dreams we tell no one
for fear we'll end up like our fathers.
Tomorrow we will rise and go out
to set another day in motion, string wires, dig holes,
beat wood and nails into living spaces, timbers
into bridges made of stone. Tonight, we sit and shiver
at the suggestions between the flames,
imagining what we could have been if we'd only
imagined more—our breaths joining
with unholy smoke permeating our leather jackets,
rising with nowhere to go we recede.

## Queen City Diner

The linoleum announces
every other footstep
of the one-legged woman
who comes to take your order.

The ketchup-stained smock,
lengthened within inches
just above her ankles,
is not enough

to hide the fact
her right leg is a wooden hinge.
Handing you a menu
she points to the parking lot,

makes you turn your head
the whole way around
to the beat-down '74 Nova
she says she bought brand new

with the settlement
from her third divorce,
then asks, *What makes you*
*so interested in cars?*

Lighting a Camel
she sits in the booth
directly across from you.
Holding the smoke

between her teeth,
she reaches below the table
and fumbles
like she's taking off a shoe.

You hear a strap pop
and buckles unclasping,
until she notices you
trying not to notice her

and asks, *Do you want to see?*
You don't make eye contact
but she's already pushing
an abrupt knee into your lap.

You're surprised
at how hard the skin
across the bone has become,
as she reaches down

and takes your hand,
tracing a circle
around the fat scar
where the doctors tied it off.

She pushes herself up
to go get your coffee,
leaving the prosthesis behind.
Then shuffle-hopping

like a busted toy,
she shouts over her shoulder
through the kitchen door,
*I'll tell you how I lost it*

*when I get back...*
And though you really want
to see how she'll manage
to not spill the coffee,

you have to make it
to Memphis by the morning,
and you've already
heard enough.

So you take the leg,
leave a $5 bill on the table,
and tiptoe, because you can,
into the unsettled night.

## Fame

This dead rabbit I found gutted
along the backyard fence
makes me wonder who among us
jumped at the chance
to join the KISS Army.
I know, it makes no sense,
but think back, remember
the make-up and grinding guitars,
the stage-act-schlock of a demon,
a lover, a cat and a spaceman,
thrown together as band-fellows,
as only glam-rock allowed.
Who wouldn't have given
anything for the chance
to be a rock star, the bronzed glory
of being rich and adored?
Unlike most classic rock bands
here was a genuine opportunity—
the anonymity of face-paint,
the fire-breath, and spit blood—
all summed up in the photo
of the drummer (he was the cat)
taking off his wig after a show.
The ridiculous long hair flowed
around his shoulders like a veil,

but beneath the back-stage lights
the crown of his bald head
glimmered with sweat.
Any one of us could've made it,
because now it was all about
*Rock and roll all night, Get up*
*everybody's gonna move their feet,*
and didn't seem to require any talent
at all. Which led to daydreaming
and *becoming* your favorite,
led to the affection for all things
black, closed doors, and *borrowing*
your mother's make-up.
Then in the shower, removing
the evidence, shouting the lyrics
to *Cold Gin, Strutter* and even *Beth,*
that supplanted math equations
you should have memorized
for tomorrow's homework,
so out of tune and off-key
that anyone passing
would have thought a baby bunny
was being ripped apart somewhere.
Which brings me back
to this dead rabbit, in case
you thought I forgot. It's been lying
by the fence all this time,
waiting to be discovered all along.

James Benger

## Dried

This was supposed to be temporary;
just a few months,
maybe a year,
till things were straightened out,
the ground was back under her,
all the rest,
all the bad parts of the past,
really all of the past,
was buried and gone.

Pulling a sun-wrinkled shirt from the line,
bare dirt beneath her flip-flops,
she reflects on how
people are really the only things that die;
the past keeps breathing new horror,
or worse,
constant repetitious banality.

The elastic band on her underwear's
still a little damp,
but she takes it down anyway
because if soggy shorts were anything but
the least of her worries,
life would be something other than hers.

She takes the basket,
now fully loaded,
back inside the single-wide
with the cracked kitchen window.
She doesn't much care
if the shirts ever get folded.

## The Modern Age

They're sitting around
a rotting out picnic table
out back, but somewhat adjacent
to all four trailers.

No coolers needed;
the sixers never last long enough
to get cold,
and they rock/paper/scissors
(in the later rounds, smear the queer)
for who has to go inside
and supply the next.
All of their fridges are fully stocked
of everything but food.

Crumb snatchers in bed
and ladyfolk in front of the tv
or the dishes
or bed
or out with (we won't think about that),
they hold court,
talk about the real matters.
The Communist threat,
the Coloreds,
their undocumented arsenals.

One wifey stumbles barefoot
to the tableside and informs her other
that the a.c.'s out again.
He advises her to get her
bitch ass back inside,
'fore he blacks her other eye.
The congregation laughs their approval
as she brokenly shuffles back to the
aluminum sweatbox, failing to hide the tears.

Once she's inside,
the lovers of life
crack another
and toast to the modern age.

## Stagnant

There are reasons to keep moving.

That's what she keeps telling herself,
but everything keeps getting
paper thin,
water thin,
flaccid,
impotent,
useless,
a waste.

Nothing has that fire,
that potency,
that urgency,
that importance.

The unnamed stains
on the chipped Formica countertop
tell her all she needs to know
about how old, yet un-sepia
her world has gotten.

She goes to the plastic blinds in the front window,
once neutral beige,
now cemented in thick dust.

The kids are paying in the dirt.
She used to be that,
back when all of this
wasn't so crushingly depressing.

There's a knife in the kitchen drawer;
the shiniest, prettiest thing in the trailer,
she includes herself in that estimation.

*Cafe* by Josh Crow

Kerry Trautman

## To a Friend Who Moved to Florida II

We know blizzards—their white
oblivion beyond our windows.

You cowered in your girlhood basement while
a tornado growled over your house.

We know broken
glass and fences,
blackout, flood and lightning.

But this—
this hurricane Irma wider than your Florida
dangling into hot fuel ocean like
a child's stray toe tempting under-bed monsters—
this is new.

This could swallow your new life,
take you further from me
than you already flew.

You wait, collect
batteries, water bottles,
shutter windows with dark steel for
three days of waiting in dark.

I watch swirl-color CNN maps
trace projected paths with
fingertip on the screen
resting there
your town below my fingertip, shielded.

## End-of-Season Sestina

My twin maples won't be swayed.
They know their glow—orange-red—
means they'll be dead soon. The birds
perched on topmost branches shiver,
leaves disappear, harder to hide.
Once familiar tree becomes a stranger.

All bodies gradually become stranger
to ourselves. A cow becomes suede.
No fur to stroke, but only hide.
No lowing in fields, but skin, red
meat, leather. With a shiver
bodies succumb to weather. Birds

leave their leaves, flown south. Birds'
nests blown to brown grass. Stranger
still from inside the house, we shiver
wrapped in wool afghans, on suede
sofa, all these former bodies, like unread
books no longer mean themselves. They hide

former lives behind exposed hides.
Come April the skull of a bird
will shimmer ivory among red
tulips, a bony exposed stranger
among fluttery bulbs that sway
in rainsweeps. Do skulls shiver?

And if skulls then do femurs, ribs, shiver
the way animal or human hide
will then, still warm and swayed
by blood and sunlight, turning to bird-
song? Clinging to the hand of a stranger
to both avoid impending red

death? A book can't know it's unread.
Spine intact with dusty shiver
in shelves awaiting thumbs of strangers
licked for pages, it hides,
drying like a bird's
egg in fallen nest. Trees will sway

regardless of birds' nests, barks shiver
too and red leaves can't hide.
unswayed by death who's no stranger.

## Salt-Tooth

The sweet ones are forgiven their
obvious leanings toward
toffees or meringue.
Indulging a craving for caramel
is justly becoming of a lady—
respecting human mastery over
sugar cane and cassia bark,
kitchen scientists tempering chocolate
for the greater good.

But you,
insolent saboteur,
coerce my tongue toward fat-cut
French fries oozing peanut oil and
doused in malted vinegar.
You beg the crystalline flakes
hiding in bites of aged English cheddar.
Or the crisp of taquitos.
Or the yielding of a calzone crust to what
it wraps, hot, in its garlic-dusted belly.
Or soft chili dogs handed thru the
car window by a summer-job 16-yr-old.

Shhhh, my salt-tooth friend,
salivating urges ancient as survival,
inborn as a lust for fire-charred meat.

Don't remind me of
the shape of my animal teeth,
that BBQ sauce and gravy and ketchup are
but flavor-cousins of blood.

Paul Koniecki

## Flying over Milwaukee

*-for Bobby Koch*

My parents had the same
house for forty-nine years.

You happened to be outside
just across the street the

day I took my kids
to see it. As you stood

in your parents yard like
you were waiting for a

bell to ring I said
look kids it's Bobby Koch

The King of Wisconsin and
I thought about how you

were as bald now as
a missed free throw but

I didn't say it. I
choose to remember instead how

you started for the varsity
basketball team in the ninth

grade and how glad I
was you didn't have a

pot-belly or a cane
and how playing in your

parent's drive way once on
a warm summer night with

the wind at your back
a long time ago yesterday

I saw you jump all
the way over the moon.

## harry dean stanton says i can remember him anyway i want

my maternal grandfather's
given name was jerome

but everyone called him harry
grandma ann sang i want that man

i cant answer for the dean part or
anything beyond my own bad choices

but if you knew ann then you'd have
seen he never stood a chance

it's an understatement
to say that i am jealous

of the painters and the actors
and the sculptors self-evidently

covered in each day's miraculum
knowing i'd give anything

for a studio of my own
to have something to come out from

i even put on a bowler
and an eye patch before

i sat down just now only to find
nothing helps this poem

## Last Night I Saw John Fante

before the end in a dream,
his not mine.

Or Josh Weir.

A healthy younger man explaining
the gravity of whiskey

and reading Delmore Schwartz
flat as a broom

on the floor
having missed the chance

to catch something
as solid as the wall.

Last week he called me
from a public pool in

Midland, Texas surrounded
by splashing children

shouting I'll get you little
heathens and a poem

he had just written
for the Princess of Bunker

Hill or South America. We
laughed at Facebook

phone
reception and I read him
my latest poem too. The

air crackled
drunk with words and love.

*Annabel* by Josh Crow

Michael Hackney

## Sliver of Advice

Tumbling down to the enduring sea,
nevermind the design of things, fathered by still hours;
nevermind the delicate flower, the hungry beast;
work until last-light settles over your brittle bones;
and breathe one last breath, before diving into the cold
water...

drowning ever the need for just causes.

## Whatever Be Blessed

Now the day
with too much
red in it,
the lamplight
cutting the eyes
like ammonia.
Now the night
with no end,
no housecoat
long enough
to cover me,
no evening charm...
nothing
but the carcasses
of left-over poems,
rendered in blood
and agonized over.

## Weekend

The chanting, the hypnosis,
and the actual enlightenment
take place in my living room
on a Sunday afternoon.
Then, some serious dipping
into Trautman's poetry collection
where wise, picturesque phrases
take hold and do not let up...
This morning, I was flattened out
like a tortilla, my throat parched
from Saturday evening's cigar
and celebration at a downtown,
upscale establishment,
where obvious men flirted
with blond-headed waitresses...

And what of you?
Did you run into any red weather?

## Marybeth Niederkorn

### The Moon Rocks Over

The hillside's dewy tonight, and cold
while the moon rocks over us all. I haven't
seen the stars so sharp as they are tonight
in years. It's as though they're seeing me
as much as I'm seeing them, with new clarity,
which is a touch unsettling to speak the truth on
the subject. But the moon rocks over us all
and softens imperfections daylight seems
to revel in revealing. I could watch it do its
thing for hours on end, never once looking away,
which is the biggest advantage the moon has
over the sun, in my estimation, though the night
has appeals beyond the soft moon and diamond-
bright stars, they shine while the moon rocks
over us all. The cattle low and grasses rustle while
I stand watching, thinking. It's how I do, long hours
feel slower, long thoughts go deeper, and I feel myself
pulling into the hillside almost as much as it's pulling
into me while the moon rocks over us all.

# Highway 32 West

They say a journey of a thousand steps begins with a single mile, or maybe I have that wrong, but it feels right, on this stretch of 32 that has no shoulder but plenty of logging trucks. I can picture myself catapulting end over end into the sedge and pine forests on either side of the highway, one side bisected by railroad tracks, the other with its furrowed valley that I get a vague sense of disapproval from. I'm not sure if I'm projecting. I'm not sure of much, here, with my travel mug of lukewarm coffee and my radio turned all the way down because the static is almost worse than the country music or the station out of St. Louis that *You never know what you'll hear next!* which sounds more than a little ominous, to me. Or maybe I'm picking up on the rage coming at me from the redneck in his dooley pickup truck. Spellcheck tells me dooley isn't a word, and Google is pretty sure I mean *dually,* but search results seem to be telling me that a *dually* pickup truck is not what I assumed a dooley was, i.e., a pickup truck with dual wheels in back, often accompanied by chrome truck nuts, I reckon. *Truck nuts,* I might add, are a thing I assumed *had* to be fictional, since I first saw them on a cartoon show about redneck debauchery, which has some elements of satire, but no, no, *truck nuts are real.* People really do set out with the sole purpose of getting their hands on a dangly set of faux testicles to hang from their truck's trailer hitch, and then they just kind of drive around with them on, maybe yelling *WOOEEE!* more frequently than your average driver, because he's behind the wheel of a dooley pickup truck, freshly gross from muddin'. It's a lifestyle choice, I guess, one that also involves shouting obscenities at a blonde in a sedan who drives the speed limit, *sensibly.* Like, aggressively sensibly.

Not that I mind being screamed at by a man whose bumper stickers carry vile messages, who probably wouldn't scream at me in any other context, unless I was walking alone on a street. Then probably he'd take it upon himself to remind me that damn, my hot ass is hot, and he thanks me for leaving the kitchen so he could see it. From across the street. Where I can't punch him. Because *courage* is totally in this guy's wheelhouse. Yeah, scream at the driver ahead of you with the staff parking permit for a community college. Yeah, scream at the driver whose car is clearly just this side of falling completely apart, as evidenced by the missing bumper cover and by the giant dent from where some damn kid was out skateboarding (probably) and fell on the hood, which crumpled like a paper sack, but more expensively. Yeah, scream at the driver who isn't moving slowly solely to piss you off, but who is acutely aware of those logging trucks, and of the farm-implements sales yards (plural) between here and the next major highway. It's not that I want to rear-end a combine, or a tractor with a back-end loader whose metal spikes are bigger around than my leg, and would be aimed directly into the driver's seat, where, you might have noticed, *I happen to be sitting.* I guess I think about things that other people maybe don't consider while they're trying to run over the chick in the Honda.

## Strung

The town had only five balloons,
each dark gray, filled with smoke
and income. The balloons didn't
look like much, maybe, to an
outside eye, but to us, they held
more promise than the empty
dream of America.

The balloons were tied to heavy
black strings, long, so long they
seemed to disappear into heaven,
but we all knew better. They were
our beacon to the world, our
call to other businesses. *Come,*
our balloons said. *We are above*
*a viable place.*

Until the first string broke, we
were doing fine. The first, the
next, the last. Fine. At least that's
what we told ourselves in the
face of pollution the companies
wouldn't clean. The money ran
dry, along with the pensions,
along with the tax revenue
that paid for bridges in
and out.

We still have our strings, feet
tangled in their damp twisted
heaps, and the more we try
to work our way out, the more
they weave into a choking
net.

Maybe we'll catch another.

*Dream House* by Alison Erazmus

## Joseph Davis

### Dancing Alone at the Edge of the Universe

So many times in so many ways I will saddle myself with the pettiness of evil. And when looking for shelter from that venial or mortal burden of evil exhausts me, and I manage to look past the hypocrisies, betrayals and dogmas of belief, disbelief and unbelief I have wastefully stretched my reality into, I am dancing alone at the edge of the universe.

A dance of exhilaration and healing, I kick up cosmic dust and asteroids while laughing loudly in the newly known umbra of Pluto. Such moments come in the burst of a milkweed pod, the wind blowing on my bare feet in bed, even in the tiresome toil of busing tables — even then, this dance is very lucid, very real, transcending the tedium by leaps and bounds.

There must be a glint of malice in an atheist,
who, while rejecting the notion of someone or
something bigger than our absurd and bumbling selves,
still recognizes that inextinguishable spark of
greed and licentiousness, and gathering humanity into
mindless, dictated herds. And the cosmos only knows
how many righteous tongues of fire —

apparently ignited by brimstone — replicate in a mind replete with the Pharisees' religiosity: twisted deeds and atrocities done in the name of god, who seems to require two-thirds majority to pave that well-intentioned road to paradise.

Astronomical in their extreme success, *isms* of both ilks simply want to engulf the universe in that gaping gyre that first frightened poor falcons and desert birds.

But somewhere that farthest star we take in with our beady little eyes IS a source, un-stratified, un-annihilated by dictums of dogma. And once we've hacked ourselves and that farthest star into the bite-sized oblivion we were craving, perhaps that source will try and swallow us, only to belch and spew all prime matter and back into the very cosmos of pure potentiality we cringed from in the beginning.

But until that time comes, I content myself with dancing alone at the edge of the universe.

## john wayne in the ghetto

when john wayne rode so tall in the saddle
in the little black and white box later clouded by color,
we didn't cringe in awe or fear

we hissed our outrage

daddy would snap the newspaper
and without even looking up
*turn that stuff off son and sit back from that television*

john wayne doing the cowboy thing
could actually make mama pop her chewing gum
in disgust, and when she rolled her eye that one
certain way ...? hell even the marlboro man couldn't
mess with that!

mama and daddy knew the little black and white box
transmitted hidden deceptions meant to destroy little
black boys, such as a white man like john wayne
being proud of his plunder and prejudice

john wayne, oh so tall in the saddle
in the colored cube of illusion
didn't make me proud to be an american
and i damn sure didn't want to be no cowboy
i just wanted to kick john wayne's racist ass;

he made jeering a *chinaman* or killing an *injun* so cool
by simply riding off into the technicolor sunset,
so macho and chic, with that rugged *je ne sai qua*
that made hate as fashionable as alcoholism and
emphysema

oh yeah, hollywood put john wayne in the little black
and white box, made him ride oh so tall in the saddle
that he made us laugh laugh laugh here in the ghetto
while other folk somewheres else
laughed every bit as hard at amos and andy

## Summer Notes

as you sit and slowly rock on the front porch swing
listening to the momentous wisdom of thunder
and the prophetic catharsis of driving rain,
remember beauty

and when you hear the song of cicadas
ricochet among the trees, tired and heavy
under their blessed burden of green,
remember peace

creation's grace will make you giddy
when you bite into the ripe and reddest peach
and if you don't have a napkin
to catch the juice dripping from your chin
the universe will understand

watch the fireflies rise from cut and uncut lawns
to herald the sultry solitude of night,
and remember gratitude

> and I love watching you gaze at the birds
> scattering like jacks tossed from a child's
> sticky hand because you never cave in
> to that nameless fear that tried to invade
> our serenity here

because compassion thrives in summer
like lovers on their way home to make sweat and
babies under the humid moon while brooding
pigeons are cooing their approval in simmering
syncopation to the raucous roundelays of crickets

## Gary Lechliter

### Horsefly

*On wrongs swift vengeance waits.*

-Alexander Pope

The fucker I smacked and left to die,
belly up on the ground, waits for
the labor of ants to carry it off.
It's not unlike the one that blooded
me as I played in my grandmother's
garden hose on a summer day.

That one made off with boy flesh.
And all I could do was weep and howl,
which brought my father out to the
lawn, where he chased it with the
newspaper's help wanted ads,
but could not smack the villain.

So now I must call this menace
I've flattened an icon of vengeance
and leave it in the mulch, where
the widow and fatherless grubs
will come to honor the knowledge
that only fools linger.

## Road

*If, where fire and smoke are thickest, there's no work for you to do...*

—Ellen M.H. Gates, 1860

Take this narrow dirt road,
wheels rattled on the cattle-guard,
past the creosote fence-posts
lit by low angles of the sun.
Drive past the aged bales, once
round, shagged and wooly.

Take this winding backroad
because you know it endures,
because the local grader pushed
rocks to brace your wheels
from the far side of the ditch,
holes from years of combines
and trucks to haul the corn.

Take this washboard road
with your window down to the
wind and leaves that catch your
face unaware, that wing their
flight like birds, hitchhiking
under your windshield wipers.

Take this one-horse road
and don't care a thing about it,
because it holds sure passage
where spent leaves cast their
fire and smoke, dust of ash,
hard winter coming.

## Photos of Ghosts

*for Charles Simic*

Come back tonight in the snow.
You left your watch and fly swatter
by the kitchen sink, where flies
swarm above the dishwater, those
bad guests of winter, inside for soup
and crackers to warm the gut.

Come back to the pantry with your
can-opener, or we'll surely faint from
hunger, and not be ourselves for days.
Stand by the table that was given
to us those decades ago, when
our love and the house was new.

You're barely gone and you miss
me still. What's it been 10 seconds?
Your hat and coat hang dusty
in the hall like you never left.
And all the mirrors, with photographs
of ghosts, hold no image of you.

*Furs Found* by Alison Erazmus

## James Brubaker

### Twenty-Seven

Reeves is screwing the motel maid when Kay gets back from the free continental breakfast. Kay slams the door and asks Reeves what the fuck he's doing.

"What does it look like I'm doing?" he says.

That's the only answer he offers until he finishes. This doesn't take long because every time he thrusts, the maid bites his cheek and does this thing with her fingernails on his shoulder blades. If he hadn't been so close to getting off, Reeves would have quit out of courtesy toward his wife, even though they've had this arrangement—that he's allowed to mess around when he's on tour—for most of their marriage. When the agreement was reached, Kay wasn't regularly coming along on tours, but Reeves sees no need why her presence should change anything, and Kay never asked him to stop. Anyway, had Kay remembered to leave the Do Not Disturb sign on the door when she left for breakfast, the maid never would have walked in to find Reeves getting out of the shower, nor would she have recognized him from the Blood Blister videos that used to be all over MTV back in the 90's.

Reeves pulls out when he finishes, grunts and rolls onto his back. He spots the maid's name tag.

"Thank you, Erika," he says.

She gathers her uniform and puts herself together

on her way out the door. Reeves isn't sure if she's in a hurry because she's embarrassed at Kay's intrusion, or annoyed that he finished before her.

"You're a dick," Kay says, when Erika is gone.

Reeves lights a cigarette, drops the spent match on his sweaty chest. He knows Kay is right.

"It's better than being dead," he says.

*

Truthfully, Reeves kind of wishes he were dead. Not in the way frustrated people say things like, "I wish I were dead," or, "I'd be better off dead." He thinks his life would have been better had he died young, maybe thirteen or fourteen years ago, when he was twenty-seven, right after Blood Blister released their third album, *Half Empty,* to critical acclaim. Back in '97, the band was still pulling down headlines in *Rolling Stone* and playing packed arenas. That's the right time to go out, like that thing Cobain said in his suicide note about burning out and fading away. Of course, there was also that other line in the same note, the bit where Cobain talked about being an erratic, moody baby. Reeves understands both sentiments, but he never found a way to get to the dying, so he usually feels like an erratic, moody baby. He didn't want to be another suicide so close to Kurt's, so he bided his time, kept drinking hard and doing drugs, and then, before he knew it, he was forty, married, barely interested in music, and rarely interested enough to smoke a joint let alone time himself off.

Sometimes he still talks about killing himself, but Kay can talk him out of it by pointing out that people wouldn't see his death in a romantic, young-rock-star kind of way, but in a washed-up-dull-asshole kind of way.

"You missed your window for suicide," she says.

"You're going to have to do better than that at this point," she says.

When Reeves asks what he could possibly do now to go out in style, Kay will think for a moment. The thinking bothers Reeves because her answer is always the same. The entire exchange is pure theatre.

"Keith Moon," she says. "Or a plane crash. Unless you can get someone to kill you. But let's face it, you're no John Lennon."

*

By the time Reeves and Kay show up at the Blind Pig, the rest of the band has finished loading in for sound check. Reeves is tuning his guitar when the promoter—a kid in his mid-twenties—approaches him, tells him that ticket sales have been lukewarm so far, but he hopes things will pick up at the door.

"There isn't much going on in town, tonight," the kid says, "and a lot of the rock kids don't like to buy tickets in advance."

"Long as we get the guarantee," Reeves says.

He is used to lukewarm ticket sales. That doesn't mean he is happy about low headcounts, only that he has accepted them. Last week in Cincinnati, Blood Blister played to twenty-six paying customers in a small bar. Two nights ago in Bloomington, they were up to forty-three. Still, the band gets a minimum of a grand a night—this is a nice guarantee, but not great, a show of good will based on past successes. Some nights, this makes Reeves feels like a con man. He takes the money anyway because the band needs to get paid. Two weeks into a five week tour, Blood Blister have only played two gigs where they earned more than the minimum. Most nights, promoters and venues lose money. It's only a matter of time before the shows dry up or the guarantees go down. But that's what happens when a band's most recent album is three years old and went largely unnoticed upon release.

*

Blood Blister takes the stage before midnight. Through their first three songs, Reeves does not acknowledge the rest of his band. They're serviceable musicians, but the thought of filling out a band that was once a raw and volatile machine with competent professionals disgusts him. When the feedback dies down from the third song, a slightly sped up version of "Banger's Burns"—an early, not-quite-hit that got some radio play in ninety-one—Reeves steps up to the microphone to introduce his backup band.

As he introduces each member, the crowd boos. This is normal. The audiences know that the band's original lineup is long gone, but they still register their dissatisfaction at not experiencing the original Blood Blister. The jeers don't bother Reeves. He takes them as a sign of his band's former successes. Of the original members, the drummer, Dan Roodhouse started his own group in 2001, a pop punk outfit called E.T. that achieved modest success on the radio, and are currently enjoying a sold-out Midwest club tour. And the original bass player, Topher Anguire, died from a heroin overdose a decade ago. Every night when Reeves introduces his new bass player, a rent-a-side-man named Steven Snyder, to a generous union of boos, Reeves can't help but envy Topher. He was the smart one.

*

Between the end of the band's set and their unprovoked encore, Reeves does a shot of Southern Comfort. A minute later, back on the small stage, playing "Ampheta-mean," Blood Blister's second most successful, but most beloved-by-fans song, and looking out over the thirty or forty bored patrons who aren't crowding toward the door, Reeves thinks of those old pictures of Janis clutching a bottle of SoCo in her fist while wailing guttural blues at her audience, how, like Topher, she died doing heroin at the Landmark Motor Hotel in Los Angeles. Only, Topher died in his apartment in Portland.

*

"You didn't use a condom this morning," Kay says, back at the hotel after the show.

"I pulled out."

He knows his poor excuse will only provoke Kay further. Part of the agreement for their open marriage is that they always use protection when not with each other. Reeves almost never uses condoms, but has managed to hide this from Kay until this morning when she saw his transgression with her own eyes. He knows this is one rule he should never break for Kay's sake, but he can't help himself.

"AIDS isn't a good rock star death," Kay says.

"She didn't have AIDS."

Kay continues, listing Freddie Mercury and Fela Kuti and that guy from the Bhundu Boys.

"Those aren't romantic deaths," she says.

"It bums people out," she says. "No one wants to watch a rock star get sick and wither away."

*

After Kay falls asleep, Reeves goes for a walk and smokes a joint, lit with his white lighter. It's always a white lighter. Reeves doesn't believe that the lighter will cause his death—despite the myths that Jim, Jimi, Kurt and Janis were all in possession of white lighters when they died—but he clings to the superstition, anyway.

The band's motel is on the outskirts of Ann Arbor, situated between strip malls and chain restaurants. Reeves walks on the side of the road past the businesses, up onto an overpass. He doesn't know the interstate stretched below, into and out of the early morning darkness.

Occasional trucks and travelers appear as specks of light in the distance, become a rush of air beneath the bridge and are gone. Reeves could jump and be done with things, easy like that.

"What's the point, though?" he imagines Kay asking.

And she's right—a forty-year-old rock star is still a forty-year-old rock star whether he's playing to thirty people in a dive bar, or dead on an interstate. Anyway, Reeves notes, the overpass isn't high enough to kill him. He'd have to fall and wait for a car or truck to finish the job. He doesn't have that level of commitment.

*

"You could do a Paul McCartney and we can become vegetarians and you can write clever sentimental songs about domestic life," Kay says. She's eating Cheerios out of a Styrofoam bowl in the motel lobby. This is how she tries to convince Reeves to be a better husband. To convince him that rock stars can age gracefully--like Sting, and Eric Clapton, and Bono, and Phil Collins, Kay will say. Reeves thinks they all suck now, and he knows that Kay knows they suck, so he decides to argue.

"That's not even Paul McCartnety," he says.

Kay is annoyed as Reeves begins listing the alleged clues of Paul's death peppered through The Beatles' late albums—the palm of death over Paul's head, his being dressed as a corpse on the cover of *Abbey Road,* the infamous, slowed down "I bury Paul," from the end of "Strawberry Fields Forever," the "28 IF" license plate.

"They were saying cranberry sauce," Kay says. "And he would have been twenty-nine."

*

After Michigan, the tour takes the band to Philadelphia. Blood Blister's set starts early, to forty people. They aren't headlining. That honor is reserved for a local act, a guy with a guitar and a sequencer who plays novelty songs. Reeves mumbles through the set, strumming behind the beat on every song while he scans the room for mildly attractive, lonely looking women he can try to bang in the bathroom after the show. Anymore, it isn't unusual for Reeves to be distracted on stage. The band's early momentum kept gigs exciting for a few years, but now he's only carrying on because he doesn't know what else to do. Some gigs—one gig out of twenty, maybe—the crowd will be just right, and this makeshift version of Blood Blister will coalesce into something raw and exciting, and Reeves will feel like he felt when the band was new. This is not one of those nights. Tonight, Reeves is only interested in trading his waning celebrity for a piece of ass.

Kay decided not to come to the show tonight. She needed a night off from the noise, but Reeves suspects she's still upset about his quickie with the maid the other day. He can't really fault her for that. Though their relationship has been open since they were married, they are both getting old. Kay hasn't had an affair in five years and is talking about having kids.

Reeves isn't surprised that she's pissed. She has every right to be. The only reason Reeves fucks around on Kay anymore is because he can. Like the music, the thrill of banging groupies isn't what it used to be. Anymore it is an exercise in habit or muscle memory.

Reeves spots a couple of women on the floor as he muddles through a song—the name of which he can't even remember—from Blood Blister's latest album. There's a shapely woman in her early forties, smoking near the front. She's wearing a denim skirt and a leather jacket. She bobs her head to the songs and once or twice raises her arms and tries to dance. There's another woman, a girl practically, wearing an old Blood Blister t-shirt from ten years ago, sitting at a table by herself in the corner. She rests her face on her palms—probably a college student, too smart and too sensitive for what Reeves wants. She'll be his back-up.

As the set progresses, one tired song after another, the room slowly fills. By the end of the set, the room is packed with two hundred bodies and the last song gets only a smattering of applause. There will be no encore tonight, as Blood Blister is not headlining. This does not bother Reeves. Most of the time encores only prolong Reeves's boredom at being up on stage. When the set ends in a wash of unintentional feedback, Reeves leaves his guitar behind and heads straight to the bar. He orders a SoCo on the rocks and sets out to look for the women he spotted earlier.

*

The woman in the black leather jacket's name is Moira. She won't fuck in the cramped men's room in the bar's back corner, but does not mind the back of a tour van filled with amps, guitars and a drum set. While Reeves moves some gear around to make room, she tells him that she's got two kids. They live with her ex so she only sees them twice a month. This is her weekend, she tells him, but she left them with one of her girlfriends so she could get out. This admission disgusts Reeves. He considers telling Moira she's a terrible mother and a worse human being and sending her off. He doesn't send her off, though, because why bother?

Once Reeves is done moving gear around, Moira climbs in ahead of him, plants her elbows on an amp, and hikes up her skirt. Reeves crawls in behind her, closes the van door and pulls a condom out of his wallet.

"You clean?" Moira asks.

"Far as I know," Reeves answers.

"So am I," she says. "And I'm tied. She adds,

"If you don't want to waste a rubber."

Reeves digs under his thumbnail with the foil edge of the condom wrapper while he tries to decide if he can trust this stranger. He tucks the condom into his pocket and unzips his fly.

"You don't even have to pull out," Moira says.

*

While the guy with the headliners finishes his set on stage Reeves nurses his fifth SoCo on the rocks and runs his hand up Moira's thigh, contemplating a second tussle in the van. Soon, as the crowd begins to filter out, Dan finds Reeves, grabs him by the wrist and pulls him outside without an explanation. As Dan leads him through the crowd, Reeves expects to see Kay at the end of the march, impatiently tapping her foot on the sidewalk, waiting to scold him for his newest infidelity.

Instead, Dan pulls him down the alley next to the bar where the van is parked. The back doors are standing open. Except for a pack of guitar strings, a single patch chord, one drum stick, and a lone gulf club, which Reeves keeps in the van for self defense, all the band's gear is gone. Dan pushes Reeves against the van's open door and grabs something out of the van.

"Did you fuck her out here?" Dan says.

"That woman, did you bring her out here?"

Reeves begins to feel sick, doesn't answer.

"Are these hers?" Dan asks, holding up Moira's black thong with a skull and cross bones on the front.

"Did you fuck her out here?"

Reeves nods.

Dan shoves the thong into Reeves's face and punches him the stomach. Shouts something about his brand new drum set and punches him again.

*

"How is it your fault?" Kay asks. She's curled up to him in bed, pulling her fingernails gently along his hip bone.

Reeves tells her he forgot to load in the box of patch chords at first and took them out after the load out then forgot to lock up. He doesn't like lying to Kay, but he isn't ready to tell her what really happened. Since the motel maid, something has changed between them, and he is afraid that by confessing his most recent infidelity he would make an already tenuous situation volatile.

"What are you going to do about it?"

"I don't know," Reeves says. "Check the pawn shops and call the insurance company."

"When's the next gig?"

"Three days from now. In Kansas."

"Shit," she says.

"Shit," Reeves says.

Then Kay asks him if he wants to fuck. Tells him that she's forgiven him for the other day.

"I don't feel good," he says. "Maybe tomorrow."

Kay turns away without saying anything. Reeves puts his hand on her shoulder and she shrugs it off. At that moment, Reeves becomes aware of an unpleasant itch and reaches down to scratch at his pubic region. He first noticed the itch earlier, but at that point it wasn't anything out of the ordinary. The itch has grown fierce since his return to the hotel. Reeves remembers that he didn't pull out, and wonders if Moira was lying about anything else.

*

Reeves sinks down in the hotel bath tub, scrubs the shampoo out of his hair with his finger tips. He got out of bed to take a bath in the hopes that the hotel's complimentary shampoo would deal with the, what he guesses are crabs chewing up his crotch. When the cheap, thin shampoo did nothing, he used the rest of the bottle on his hair. Now, he massages the suds from his submerged head and thinks about Brian Jones, discovered motionless at the bottom of his swimming pool and Dennis Wilson, bloated and grey, dredged up out of the Marina Del Ray.

Reeves bends his knees to slide down further into the tub. His mouth and nose break the water's surface. He thinks to slide a bit further, but imagines Kay telling him that drowning in a bathtub is absurd.

"At least find a nice body of water to off yourself in," she might say.

*

The next afternoon, Reeves, Steven, Dan and Kay split up to scour Philadelphia's pawn shops for the stolen equipment. Dan wanted to start looking first thing in the morning, but the others convinced him that they needed to allow the thieves a few hours to get the gear to a shop.

Reeves finds their shit in the second shop he visits. Everything is there—his own Fender Mustang, his fuzz and phase pedals, two Crest amps and Marshall cabinets, Dan's Fender p-bass, and Steven's brand new Tama Granstar drum set with a full array of Zildjian cymbals. Reeves approaches the guy behind the counter—a kid with a shaved head and shoulder tattoos peaking out from his undershirt—and tries not to scratch at his crotch as he asks when the gear came in.

The kid tells him he's not sure, that he's just starting his shift, but that the instruments are pretty fresh because they weren't in the day before.

"That's my band's gear," Reeves says.

The kid pulls out a binder, checks the status on the equipment. Sure enough, the gear was brought in that morning and won't be available for sale until it clears a probationary period during which the shop submits the list of goods to the police. Reeves marvels at his luck, wonders if the shop would have actually filed the paper work. After the kid calls the police, Reeves asks who brought the equipment into the store. The kid says he's not allowed to tell. Reeves reaches into his pocket, pulls out two twenties, slides them across the counter. The kid chuckles. Reeves adds two more twenties.

"That's all I've got," he says.

Reeves knows that finding the guys who stole his band's gear is a bad idea, but he can't help himself. The kid eyes the money on the counter and pulls a page out of the binder, Xeroxes it, hands a photocopy of a photocopy of a driver's license across the counter to Reeves. The license is blurred. Reeves stares at the inscrutable image of the perpetrators' face: grey and featureless, a dark lump like a blurred out interview subject on an investigative news show. The name—Andrew Jackson—is clear, but probably fake. The address is legible, as well—14 Vine St., Apt. 3B. Reeves suspects the address is fake, too, but decides to investigate. He calls Dan, asks him to tell Kay and Steve that he found the gear and to have them meet at the shop to talk to the police when they show up.

When Dan arrives, Reeves leaves, tells his drummer that he needs to grab a sandwich and a cup of coffee or he's going to fall asleep. He doesn't want Dan or anyone else, especially Kay, to know where he's really going.

*

Reeves's cell phone rings while he's reading a map in his car. It's Kay.

"What do you think you're doing?" she asks.

"Getting a sandwich."

"Bullshit."

Reeves doesn't say anything. The kid at the pawnshop must have told her about the driver's license. Reeves hopes the kid shows more discretion when the cops arrive.

"You can't go after this guy," Kay says.

"You'll get arrested."

"I'm only going to talk."

"You'll get killed, Reeves." She trails off at his name.

*

Reeves raps on the door at 14 Vine St., Apt. 3B, shouts for Mr. Jackson. He doesn't worry about disturbing the neighbors. The building is cracked and old, the kind of place where such outbursts aren't only normal but expected. He's got his golf club behind his back, the driver that he keeps under the seat of the van in case of emergencies. The driver has been in every one of his tour vans, waiting for a situation like this one, but hasn't been needed until now. When no one answers, he tries the knob. The chained door opens half way. He reaches the head of the golf club through the opening and slides the chain from the door.

The apartment is dark and dusty inside. Two candles burn on a small end table and the faint scent of incense tries to conceal the heavy stench of body odor, thick like rotten onions. Reeves works his way through the small apartment, around piles of clothes and unopened mail, noting unpleasant stains on the carpet and cracks in the walls. Inside, Reeves stops calling out for Mr. Jackson. Now that he's trespassing, Reeves prefers to maintain the element of surprise in case someone is home. When he knocked on the door, Reeves wanted someone to answer, wanted to find himself face to face with the man on the photocopied driver's license in his back pocket. Now, he can't help but consider the absurdity of his actions.

Reeves is in the kitchen, eyeing a sink full of rusted pans when he hears the rhythmic vibrating of a cell phone down the hall. The sound spooks him. He thinks to leave, but when the phone continues buzzing, unanswered, he follows the sound. The phone's vibrations stop as Reeves arrives at the apartment's bathroom.

He stands in the door and looks down at a dark form curled around the toilet's base. He reaches down and pulls the body—a man's—away from the toilet. An arm flops on the floor revealing a large, dark stain across the man's shirt. Reeves can't help but think of Elliot Smith after having stabbing himself twice in the chest.

Reeves respects the way Smith went out, one of the more impressive rock star deaths. But this man, is he dead? Has he been shot? Is that even blood spread across his chest? The body wasn't rigid or cold when Reeves touched it.

Reeves feels around on the wall for a light switch. When he finds one, the resulting light is dim, but enough that Reeves identifies the substance on the man's shirt as vomit, not blood. An overdose, maybe. More like Nick Drake than Elliot Smith. Reeves looks at the man's face, squeezes his eyes shut, and looks again. The man's face looks exactly like it did on the photocopy of the photocopy of his driver's license, shapeless and grey, a facsimile of a human face. Though his first impulse is to run from the barely human thing on the floor in front of him, instead Reeves kneels down, checks for a pulse. He doesn't find one, but then, he never does. He puts his ear up to the man's gray, mottled mouth, and feels rather than hears a faint breath.

In the dim light, Reeves begins to piece together the cause of Andrew Jackson's present condition—a small syringe on the floor, a glass bottle on the counter, a leather case with what looks like a doctor's prescription lying on top. This wasn't an overdose at all, at least not the kind people read about in the papers. Reeves picks up the prescription bottle, squints to read in the dim light until he finds the word he is looking for: insulin.

So this is Andrew Jackson, Reeves thinks, standing now, looking down at the man who pawned Blood Blister's gear. The man is disgusting. This is no way to die. And he might die, or he might not. Reeves will never know. Reeves knows that, if the man does die, it will be neither poetic nor nice. Reeves picks up the man's cell phone from the floor, dials 911, then leaves the apartment. Reeves feels his age. He feels his life stretched out before him. As the moment's tension subsides, Reeves, once again, becomes acutely aware of the furious itching in his pubic hair.

*

In his hotel room, Reeves plays his guitar. He is writing a song when Kay comes out of the shower, glistening, nude. She slides on to the bed, her legs curled together into an elegant ogee shape, bush peeking out from her thighs, creeping up her pelvis like delicate ivy. She asks Reeves to join her. He says that he can't, not yet.

The treatment Reeves bought for his crabs, on his way to the hotel from Andrew Jackson's, is sitting unused in a Walgreen's bag, hidden inside his suitcase. He is saving it for when Kay goes to bed. Then he will sneak into the bathroom with the bottle of Permethrin 1% and clean himself.

Kay asks him a second time for sex, implores him, reminds him that they haven't slept with each other for weeks.

"Maybe tomorrow," he says.

"Maybe I should leave," Kay says. And it's here

that Reeves understands that Kay isn't asking for sex so much as she is asking if she has a reason to stay.

Reeves doesn't know what to say so he goes back to playing his guitar. The new songs course through him in a new and foreign way, not like the songs he wrote three years ago, or even the songs he wrote twenty years ago, but like something fresh and honest and true. Kay rolls onto her belly and watches him.

She thinks the song sounds good but doesn't tell him, yet. She is glad Reeves is still alive.

For his part, Reeves is struck by her beauty, and how undeserving he is. He thinks about how Kay takes care of him for no good reason, not even bragging rights because her rock star lover is a washed-up bore, not a real celebrity. She deserves better and Reeves knows it. He knows that there have been times when Kay has been the only thing keeping him from ending up like Andrew Jackson.

"You know he was just lying there in his puke," Reeves said, taking a break from his new song.

"Maybe you saved his life," Kay said.

"I don't want to know if I did."

"You could be a hero."

"I got crabs," Reeves says a little too quickly.

He hadn't planned to tell Kay, but in that moment, he couldn't not tell her.

"The maid?" Kay asks.

Reeves shakes his head, tells her about Moira and the van, about the real way the gear was stolen.

Kay doesn't say anything. Reeves digs the drugstore bag from its hiding place and hands it to her. She reads the box and hands it back, expressionless.

"I'm going to take care of these" he says,
walking to the bathroom. "And get tested when
he get home. In case."

His voice wavers as he says this last part.

In the bathroom, Reeves washes himself then unscrews the cap of the Permethrin and spreads it around his genitals, massages it into his skin and pubic hair. Kay sits naked on the toilet, watching. While they wait for the medicine to work, Kay asks Reeves why he went after the guy who stole the gear. Reeves tells her he doesn't know, anymore. After a beat, Reeves asks Kay why she is still with him. She tells him she doesn't know anymore.

*Cat Grave* by Alison Erazmus

Victor Adam Clevenger

## sweet chili sauce on cold days when the sun stayed asleep until noon

the times of eating hot wings
on hotel sheets together
have passed

sucking on the bones
of those memories

our souls will never starve to death

## beautiful things attract beautiful things

*for belle*

a shimmer lingers

it shows me
you're not a stranger
to the dust of burning stars

if you were to tell me
you could catch a hot one
in the palm of your hands

& hold it
like a passionate heartbeat
keeping it warm until the sun rises

i'd believe you

## July 8, 2017

as a hot breeze blows up from the south
in the city that jack built

a black man sells rebel flags
for fifteen dollars to young white kids
at a gas station exit off I-44

i imagine him saying
southern pride you sumbitches

his fists full of dollars
his smile as big as their granddaddy's loathing

## K.S. Wuertz

### For Doug:
### Reconciliation

I thought you were made of some kind of metal
Hard, Strong, Cold, Unyielding Iron
Maybe Nickel-plated

The barely audible
Thump, Thump, Thump
Of a heart hidden deep
Within an empty cavern... echoing

And the spears I've thrown at you
Can't reach you
They don't even dent you

And all I need do
Is battle
With one so well-equipped.

But I watched you,
When you spoke to me one night
The moonlight streaming through you...
Transparent
You were lit with fragility

The soft, white blue light of clarity
Your heart, just below the surface
Whispered to me with a steady murmur

Then I knew that my touch
Or the sound of my voice
Could crack the smooth, shiny world of You

And if those tiny cracks
Could be inflicted by my hand

I need drop all my weapons

Because I would bleed to heal you...

## The Muck of It

I stepped through the arch of St. Paul's Cemetery
Where the stones call out with their crosses and verses
Reminding God in case He's forgotten

*I'm here.*
*No, over here.*
*I'm waiting.*
*No, me first.*

The dead don't go down quietly
So I'm digging
and digging
and digging some more
There are so many empty holes.

They lay, shoulder to shoulder
patiently waiting
for their moment of eternal rest
Really, what else do they have to do?

I call to them
infused with the voice of God –
Or so I'd once thought…

But He's stepped away these days
And I think He took my shovel

But God provides
I have a teaspoon -
and it's silver.

## The Little Princes

*Your Words Touch Me* You say

How can they? I think

If you only knew

I burp them out

Like frogs
they jump from me
onto the page

It is only with time
that I watch to see...

If they grow a Crown

Or just sit on lily pads
and suck down flies

*Grapes of Wrath* by Jeff Hogue

John Dorsey

## In Kansas Thinking of You

*for cherie*

ted berrigan would never text
with his fingers
along your skin
he would call you
to borrow some money or pills
he would give you some story
about how the moon looks beautiful
while sipping a pepsi
he would use strong words
& dance nude with donna dennis
on your parents front lawn
they, your parents, would offer him
iced tea & cucumber sandwiches
while talking about the moon landing
about how it seemed like a lot of work

you would sit there in flower patterned pajamas
while he told you that you deserve to have words
wrapped around you like oak trees

& all i have to offer you is the kansas wind
something of the earth
my own thoughts on love
which i know isn't much.

## Poem for Anthony Lamar Smith

the hope chests that came over
on slave ships didn't belong to sally hemings

but rich white girls
who danced in mosh pits
to john brown's body
generations before harper's ferry

tonight kansas is hanging its anthem
on the prairie wind
in grateful blood song

the spirit of st. louis is protesting
the dreams of worried lovers

no justice
no peace

hours break like bones
& fly away
on tattered wings

this river of consequence
will never get the chance
to teach its children
how to swim.

## Braddock Serenade

my father says
that he thinks my grandfather
had bunch of mini heart attacks
years before we knew
his health went south
but just kept going
like the energizer bunny
covered in factory dust
& pittsburgh moonlight

i just remember his smile
how it glowed
playing through the pain
feeding sadness into the mouth
of bellowing smokestacks
boilers of generational poverty

the blood of the roman dead
covering his work boots
staining his dentures
taking away everything
it could.

Brett Underwood

## Muted Wisdom

In the pre-dawn morning dark,
the call of the birds enraged him.
He rolled out of the hammock
and put his foot in his back pocket.
Fell face first into the stars
that contained last night's fire.
The bug bites were portals from the wild
to gather signs, messages, signals and wisdom
from the wind, the critters, the creepy crawlies
and the unheard: those shut out of the media
and board meetings.

Some of the cries of the night are muted,
but the helicopters have eyes...
and there is blood seeping into the roots.
Ants are there to gather and interpret intel.
The same willful ignorance that ignores
the medicine man puts their antennae
music on mute.

## Dusk at the Whiskey Bar

Awaiting the yogi and a cleansing cloud of smoke.
In ten minutes no one will remember this.
Look around.
Death and sore tits blow in around the door
and window frames, but the dingbats
meet it with hot air, a collective chortle
and a rehashing of falsities.

Victory is anyone's guess.
The scorecards are a mess at this point
since the tweaker pinch ran for the ogre.
A taxi runs a red. On a dirty plate,
in the bottom half of the eighth,
grenades tossed from the street food stands
taste like pineapple. No need for a fork.

Snipers have the skulls in their sights.
They're ready to strike
with every fourth ball.
The dorks do the wave
and the umpires fart in the breeze.
The medicine men are buried in popcorn
as the cavalry approaches
to rub out the village.
All intelligence is run through a universe
where a fly sits atop a water drop
on the next table.
In ten minutes, nobody will remember

## Replacing Oil, Hate And Lightning Strikes

What's got you down?
dear swift horn, dear wept tear
near grass herds on wind and that notion
of feces in your olfactory memory.

You promised to report what cow
jumped the moon.
You, the best reporter, I forgive
you and your impotent pen.
Your scabbed over inkwell.

You never did, I know, but it is fun to pretend
in that whatever wind of bovine stench, that ha ha ha.
That mooooooooooooooooo!!
Imagine that it didn't happen and she was still chuckling.
She? Yeah!!! That jolly cow!!
Oh, the joy!

In other news, imagine if sand was the sea.
Oh! We would have more glass.
Cheap glass.
Glass to break.
Glass to eat.
Glass to chug.
Glass to belch in chards.

Through bleeding lip and chipped teeth
we would learn to enjoy it.
Even to digest it.
Like we did oil and hate and genital
Friction amidst thunderstorms
and the limitless spending at box stores
with lightning bolt scars on our haunches.

Now I want that report even more.
Bay at the moon, for me.
Get wolfy. Micturate in the weed.
Piss your love in the breeze.
Take me to your cave walls
Where you explain it all.

*Beauty + Pear + White* by Jeff Hogue

Sean Arnold

## The Waitress

From the kitchen, steak-burgers hiss on the grill,
Neil Young guitar squall spills through front-of-the-
  house-speakers,
the espresso machine clangs,
steam rises from the steaming wand,
the waitress deftly handles the latte.
She floats across the wood floor,
balancing full glasses of water on the tray
so wonderfully secure in her hands.
*Can I take your order? What'll that be tonight?*
*We have beef-tip melt and mushroom bisque,*
  *and for dessert*
*we have homemade cheesecake, gooey butter cake,*
  *and more!*
Out the window a man with a light blue business shirt
  talks mildly to a woman  with a Steel Reserve
  in a brown paper bag.
The waitress's dimpled smile floats through the busy
  dinner atmosphere
I nurse a nearly empty beer as folks rub their goatees
  at a distant table
put on my pea coat and head toward the door, shuffling
  into the night.

Love, I am an onlooker here and
a surprise visitor
keeping you company at the café.
You come home at 4:30 am
where we finally sleep side by side
on a mattress made for royalty
till I rise in the morning
to wash the dishes
at a different café.

## The Dishwasher, Walking Home Late

*After Ikkyu*

You'll find me in the dark
of February's cool smog,
crouched beneath the bare trees,
taking a piss into the moonlight.
Then I walk home crookedly through the alley,
breath acrid with gin,
the juices of the restaurant soaked into my shirt.
The bar stays open after the restaurant closes
so, I don't take my leave of that place till 3:30
  in the morning
tired but with a slanted smile,
admiring the cracked city moon.

## St. Louis On Fire

The backwoods backwards twang of an inner city
 miracle
lost beneath an elm growing out of a dumpster.
I'd sit by the river, sip a bitter root and let the barges
drift towards the city
Rick smoking insatiable in my memory.

I once heard of a fight where one man pushed another
 into the river
he flailed and met his end.
There I'd bike along that dusty fall trail, find used
 needles
search for evidence, answers
men muttering about violence
the voice of streets I could barely know or comprehend.

I got lost among a woods of brick apartment buildings
 and corner shops selling hookah
a woods of brick buildings lawless rules and a landscape
shaggy with elms and sponsored community gardens
Nikes strung across telephone poles.

The city's on fire
there are warring factions
I watch the river move.

Jim McGowin

## Water for the Dead to Wade

I am a Himalayan landscape,
dreaming layered mountainous biome,
stitched from a multitude of ghosts &
the solemn sky burials of holy strangers,

Consuming the occult of text,
cut up beyond time's boundary scab,
woven into & out of inalterable scrutiny.

An image overlaid by maddening visions
beyond all contradictions,
avalanching into these winding pages,

The sum of all thought,
wrought in eternally harmonious plexus,
mending the insanity of the waters that
flow through this particular gap in apology,

Plunging its depths reversed into the sky,
where the fish become clouds
drifting in the wind &
the key strokes are lightning strikes,

Kinetic as the strategy of snaking,
splitting the jagged peaks into premonitions,
clinging, cragged & impossibly tranquil,
each unique, each emphatic, &

Every last one of them
pointing in the same direction.

## Little Things I've Only Dreamt Of

I have taken to heart everything,
but still the umbra is too unwilling
to watch a smile that occult
fade so swiftly
into a diminishing crescent.

And it is truly a cunning form
for your neck to turn
like my own moon does,
expectantly at the sound of
a door unlatching,
letting in just enough light
to lure a daring peck,

Where I hunger for and eat
all the fingers of your thin branches
setting free the hanging stars,

Letting them finally
stay up there on their own,
unbound and appeased,
drunk on the convenience of loft,

As your new armless botany
grows entangled
into my dreaming machine,
promising to block every window,

Only instead,
falling out of my head like
words about unadorned torsos,
leaving me to wonder if
I have deep enough fingers
to pick them all up,

Exquisite little things
that they are.

## Preacher

Because we have the ignorance of
cutting the dead too deeply
when passing through them would be nothing,
we are abandoned to stretch the street level view
into something to be paid out in darkness.

This spiral is a wasteful anticipation to banishment.

I will preach while on fire,
or wonder as I pay:
*Do we always have to burn*
*in the shape of a pleasure?*

Since I cannot tense these wings hard enough
to cheat the mound,
& since the eyes are forged from nothing
but quiet ablation,
I will swear to dream in only
a few necessary colors,

Because there are indications of easy birds
in your voice
& their interlacing is sometimes like
wearing a forgery.

We rely on these thoughts of
overwrought footprints,
sometimes heavy as smoke.

Some friendly words of advice:
*Do not walk there first.*

*A Letter to Warren Rosser* by Jeff Hogue

Ken Brown

## Outlaw's Hardball

I'm playing the game from
a field which yields nothing
but backbreaking hack-work
for snack foods
with pockmarked face from
blackheads; acne—
too much cheese and spongy liver...
Musty shelter, quick evictions,
nightmares, days without erections...

All for the sake of metaphors
I once had lofty hopes and goals for —
pissed away weirdly
as years passed in chaos
with second hand holes in
old boots deep in cold slush...

Too many capers with unfriendly coppers.
Gentle-souled comrades
decomposing before me—
knee-deep in prison lice
bodies all itchy—
their craniums absolute applesauce, buddy—
and *no fucky fucky, friend. No fucky fucky.*

## Alas, Another Discovery

Hath the rose swayed 'neath the ads
whilst cruising upon, looking to see the
flying ernes — Lake Erie —
As the reel pealed tintinnabulating
I felt ill wearing the sari
So I lopped the mop top off the waif as we pulled
into the shore skyline — I was working for the CIA
and ashes abounded everywhere.

Then this colony from Taiwan holding whips started
prattling incessantly. They were murdering Zero Mostel
and his casket was molded with an ETA of crying
about it later if you didn't say anything.

I was a user at the time with a gag in my bag and
an unspoken bias — and I didn't have an iPod
every motherfucking hour —

I was idle sans the capacity to write an ode.
So, I ordered up a plate of nan —
it started snowing —
And then I threw pub darts.

## Four Religions

Kamikaze moths had tossed themselves
into a candle of bewilderment to
die for their ideas spawned
were mountains dew on grass where
rams roamed showing those who watched
precisely how to be alone and feel lightning
struck the apple Eve engorged
to change the morals charging after
those who chose to cheat or steal all
that's living how he's not destroys
the man performing for what's loathed
to earn his needed meals.

Annette Hope Billings

## Just Shy of Stars

A brown girl wanders amber waves;
a gold garland of woven wheat
crowns her head of defiant curls.
Chest tight with longing,
she scours fields for any of Kansas
that bears likeness to her.

Serenaded by meadowlarks,
she kneels to smell rich county soil,
brushing the ground
with her Cupid's bow mouth,
lips lush in a way
that makes the earth feel blessed.

She creeps up near a bison herd,
grins at their hides of richest brown.
They scatter with her cries of
*Hey you beauties, dark like me!*

A cottonwood invites her to its shade
where she lingers under summer leaves.
She stretches out and is lulled to sleep
by the lilt of honeybee buzz.

She dreams of future difficulties,
of places where she'll find
herself still just shy of stars.
Foreshadowed failures
work to startle her awake
to survey the surrounding land.

She plots a hearty stew of poems
to put meat on her Midwest bones:
its broth rendered thick
and smooth with a roux
of Gwendolyn Brooks and Langston Hughes,
of Aaron Douglas and Gordon Parks
—a stew seasoned to withstand rejection,
a plains meal to leave
her hopeful and uppity enough
to demand her hometown be more than
a good place to dig potatoes—
it must be a good place to grow
black girls too.

## Feast

She is a feast of a woman
and those who choose
to only eat salad
will miss more of her
than they will ever know.

She pays no mind
and has little time
for those who come for her
carrying tiny plates.

Her time, far too golden,
her fruit, too abundant
for those who are foreigners
to the beauty in bounty—
those unfortunate souls
who speak with such pride
of their notable passion for nibbling;
she pitys those poor souls
because she is a feast.

## Woman Well

Many exalt scarcely-tested youth
with its everything still taut, smooth,
but scant praise is heard for older women
roots deep, branches spread in power:
a woman who is a time-proven wonder
and decades from sapling status
who boasts a lush expanse of confidence,
a solid history of resilience,
and grand display of tensile strength.

Nod your head in appreciation
when you pass by where she stands,
give her foliage your full attention,
tip your hat and stand up straight,
notice leaves cascading from her
scattering wisdom in their wake.
Like a tree who has weathered many seasons,
she has aged to do *older woman* well—
still shelter, still fruit, still shade.

Sean Arnold is a poet, writer and visual artist residing in South Saint Louis, Missouri. He graduated from Webster University in 2015 with a degree in Creative Writing where he was poetry editor of the *Green Fuse* literary magazine and studied under David Clewell. Arnold is currently pursuing a Master's in Education from Webster University, and his day job is as a community support provider at a mental health agency. Previous published works include a four-part chapbook series called *Soliloquy from a Freight Yard,* which was based around freight yard romanticisms and the glorious confusion of youth. Previous publications include *Big Bridge Magazine* out of Berkley, *The Green Fuse,* and *Crossing the Divide* (an anthology created by St. Louis' poet laureate Michael Castro to promote unity through poetry). Past music credits include providing spoken word for the bands Barely Free and Holy!Holy!Holy!. For the past three years he has run a reading series out of Foam Coffee and Beer on Cherokee St. entitled Sunday Summer Spoken Word series. Arnold is a lover of dusty trails, back-alleys, freight trains, running, good health and bourbon.

Roy J. Beckemeyer is a retired engineer and scientific journal editor who lives in Wichita, Kansas. He currently studies the Paleozoic insect fossils of Alabama, Kansas, and Oklahoma, and writes poetry. His first book of poetry, *Music I Once Could Dance To* (Coal City Press, Lawrence, KS, 2014) was selected as a 2015 Kansas Notable Book. He won the *Beecher's Magazine* Poetry Contest in 2014, and the Kansas Voices Poetry Award in 2016. He recently co-edited (with Caryn Mirriam-Goldberg) *Kansas Time+Place: An Anthology of Heartland Poetry* (Little Balkans Press, Pittsburg, KS, 2017).

James Benger is a father, husband and writer. His work has been featured in several publications. He is the author of two fiction ebooks: *Flight 776* (2012) and *Jack of Diamonds* (2013), and two chapbooks of poetry: *As I Watch You Fade* (EMP 2016) and *You've Heard It All Before* (GigaPoem 2017). He is a member of the Riverfront Readings Committee in Kansas City, and is the founder of the *365 Poems In 365 Days* online poetry workshop and is Editor In Chief of the subsequent anthology series. He lives in Kansas City with his wife and son.

Annette Hope Billings is an award-winning poet and actress from the Midwest. Her dynamic style of reciting has led fans to dub her "the Maya of the Midwest." Her first book of poetry, *A Net Full of Hope* (2015), garnered the 2015 ARTSConnect ARTY Award in Literature. Her next book, *Descants for a Daughter* (2016), was a collect-ion of affirmations. Her poetry can also appears in the following anthologies: *Gimme Your Lunch Money: Heart land Poets Respond to Bullying* (2016), *Twisting Topeka* (2016), *Our Last Walk: Using Poetry for Grieving and Remembering Our Pets.*(2016), and *Kansas Time + Place: An Anthology of Heartland Poetry* (Balkans Press, 2017). Billings' poetry can also be found in both online and print publications including *Coal City Press* (2016) and *Konza Magazine* (2016 and 2017). To view short videos of her poetry performances, visit tinyurl.com/anfohvideos, her website at http://anetfullofhope.com /, her facebook: anetfullofhope, or on Twitter: @AnnetteBilling3

Dianne Borsenik is active in the northern Ohio poetry scene, and is editor/publisher at *NightBallet Press*. Her work has appeared in *Slipstream, The Offbeat, Chiron Review*, and many other magazines and anthologies. Lit Youngstown put her poem *Disco* on their tee shirts, which makes her feel like a rock star. Find her on Facebook and at www.dianneborsenik.com.

Lori Brack's Kansas roots coil down to her mother's Barton County homestead and her father's Russian-German immigrant parents. Her work background includes newspaper journalism, contemporary art education, public library programming, and college teaching. In 2010, the Field School, New York, published her chapbook *A Fine Place to See the Sky*, a poetic script for a work of performance art by Ernesto Pujol. The script is a collaboration with her grandfather's 1907-1918 Kansas farming journals.

Ken Brown was born in Missouri- left town at nineteen... Returned twenty-one years later after Minnesota, Maine, and Mississippi in a tent, Montana, Morocco- where he lived with a prostitute afflicted with polio. Normandy, Madrid, Grecian Islands- despondent- to upstate New York across the country in a Honda- through Mexico- Vegas- Santa Monica for four years doing laundry for a living then dog-sitting at the Ding Dong... Wound up in Australia-Perth- the out-bush for nine months- Hell's Angels blew up land- went broke- made ten thousand dollars on Karma Kards- fell in love for the thirteenth time- engaged-Kicked out of Australia- published in 45 periodicals- wound up back where he started.

James Brubaker is the author of *Liner Notes, Pilot Season,* and *Black Magic Death Sphere: (Science) Fictions.* His stories have appeared in various journals. Find him at jamesbrubaker.net.

John Burroughs is a nationally-touring poet and performer from the Cleveland area and the author of over a dozen books including Water Works, Electric Company, Beat Attitude and The Eater of the Absurd. His latest, Loss and Foundering, was published in Spring 2018 by NightBallet Press. Since 2008, John has served as the founding editor of Crisis Chronicles Press. Find him at www.crisischronicles.com.

When not traveling on highways across America, Victor Clevenger spends his days in a Madhouse and his nights writing poetry. He lives with his second ex-wife, and together they raise six children in a small town northeast of Kansas City, MO. Selected pieces of his work have appeared in print magazines and journals around the world, as well as at a variety of places online. In 2017, Victor was nominated for the Best of the Net Anthology, as well as the Pushcart Prize. His most recent published collections of poetry include a split book with Tom Farris titled *Ginger Roots Are Best Taken Orally* (EMP, 2018) and *A Finger in the Hornets' Nest* (Red Flag Poetry, 2018).

Daniel Crocker's work has appeared in *The Los Angeles Review, Hobart, Big Muddy, New World Writing, Stirring, Juked, The Chiron Review, The Mas Tequila Review* and over 100 others. His books include *Like a Fish* (full length) and *The One Where I Ruin Your Childhood* (e-chap with thousands of downloads) both from Sundress Publications. Green Bean Press published several of his books in the '90s and early 2000s. These include *People Everyday and Other Poems, Long Live the 2 of Spades,* the novel *The Cornstalk Man* and the short story collection *Do Not Look Directly Into Me.* He has also published several chapbooks through various presses. His newest full length collection of poetry, *Shit House Rat,* was published by Spartan Press in September of 2017. He was the first winner of the Gerald Locklin Prize in poetry. He is the editor of *The Cape Rock* (Southeast Missouri State University) and the co-editor of *Trailer Park Quarterly.* He's also the host of the podcast, Sanesplaining, about poetry, mental illness and nerd stuff. He is a bipolar, bisexual Gemini living the cliché.

Margaret Crocker is an artist, thrift store aficionado, poet, pet lover, joker and thief. She sits at the cool table and makes the best homemade pie crust in the tri-county region. She has none of the wisdom or dignity that usually comes with old age, and this makes her incredibly fun at parties.

Josh Crow is a visual artist based out of Central Missouri. A graduate of Rhode Island School of Design and Indiana University, he works on commercial, personal, and commissioned projects. With an attention to mark-making, he explores a variety of subjects through drawing and painting. He is a past alum and artist community member of Osage Arts Community. In his off time he enjoys home-brewing and archery.

Joseph Anthony Davis has lived most of his life in Kansas City, Mo, where he attended Bishop Hogan High School and went on to somehow con(vince) the monks and nuns and Benedictine College in Atchsion, Ks, to give him a B.A. in English. When not writing poetry, he tries his hand (and sometimes his voice) at music, with songwriting, composing, and the electric bass getting the most attention. He works for the Broadway District of MainCor, a *blue shirt* counterpart to the ubiquitous *red shirts* seen helping to make midtown Kansas City clean and inviting for residents and visitors alike.

John Dorsey lived for several years in Toledo, Ohio. He is the author of several collections of poetry, including *Teaching the Dead to Sing: The Outlaw's Prayer* (Rose of Sharon Press, 2006), *Sodomy is a City in New Jersey* (American Mettle Books, 2010), *Tombstone Factory,* (Epic Rites Press, 2013), *Appalachian Frankenstein* (GTK Press, 2015) *Being the Fire* (Tangerine Press, 2016), *Shoot the Messenger* (Red Flag Press, 2017), and *Letting the Meat Rest* (Spartan Press, 2017). He is the current Poet Laureate of Belle, MO. His work has been nominated for the Pushcart Prize. He may be reached at archerevans@yahoo.com

Alison Erazmus (b. 1983) is a fine art photographer, visual artist, and curator originally from the flat agricultural landscape of northern Illinois. She is currently based in Saint Louis, Missouri. She earned a Master of Fine Arts degree with an emphasis in photography from Southern Illinois University Carbondale in 2008. Since then she has exhibited her work at galleries and museums across the country, including at the South Bend Museum of Art, The Silverspace Gallery, the Cedarhurst Center for the Arts, the Evansville Museum, Art Saint Louis, the New Harmony Gallery of Contemporary Art, and the Darkroom Gallery. Her work has received honorable mentions and has been included in several juried group exhibitions, including the *Of Memory, Myth, and Bone* annual juried photography exhibition, *Light Leaked* online publication, and the Holga and Friends exhibition. She recently attended the Kimmel Harding Nelson Center for the Arts residency.

Timothy Geiger is the author of *The Curse of Pheromones,* (Main Street Rag Press, 2008) and *Blue Light Factory,* (Spoon River Poetry Press, 1999) and nine chapbooks. Other poems have appeared in such places as Poetry, America, and The Pushcart Prize XVII. He is also the proprietor of Aureole Press, a limited edition fine-press publisher housed at the University of Toledo, where he teaches Creative Writing, Poetry, and Letterpress Printing.

Mike Hackney was born in Abilene, Texas on March 20th, 1969 and was moved to Toledo shortly thereafter. In 1993, he received a BFA with a specialization in poetry from BGSU and in 2006, a MLS from the University of Toledo. He is the author of five chapbooks, four bound poetry collections and one book of essays on poetry. He has received artistic grants from the Toledo Arts Commission and The Ohio Arts Council.

Originally from the flatlands of central Illinois, Justin Hamm now lives near Twain territory in Missouri. He is the founding editor of *the museum of americana* and the author of *American Ephemeral* and *Lessons in Ruin,* as well as two poetry chapbooks. His poems, stories, photos, and reviews have appeared in *Nimrod, The Midwest Quarterly, Sugar House Review, Pittsburgh Poetry Review,* and a host of other publications. Recent work has also been selected for *New Poetry from the Midwest* (2014, New American Press) and the Stanley Hanks Memorial Poetry Prize from the St. Louis Poetry Center.

Steve Henn wrote *Indiana Noble Sad Man of the Year* (Wolfson Press 2017) and *And God Said: Let there be Evolution!* (NYQ Books 2012). He teaches high school and dads it up.

Mike James has been widely published in magazines throughout the country in such places as *Cake, Laurel Review, Negative Capability, Birmingham Poetry Review,* and *Chiron Review*. His eleven poetry collections include:

*Crows in the Jukebox* (Bottom Dog), *My Favorite Houseguest* (FutureCycle), and *Peddler's Blues* (Main Street Rag.) He has served as an associate editor for the *Kentucky Review* and *Autumn House Press*, as well as the publisher of the now defunct *Yellow Pepper Press.* He makes his home in Chapel Hill, North Carolina. More information can be found on his website at mike.jamespoetry.com.

Currently based in Dallas, Paul Koniecki's latest books of poems are, *After Working Hours* from NightBallet Press, *Reject Convention* by KleftJaw Press, and *Tom Farris is my Safe-Word* from CWP Collective Press. He was once chosen for the John Ashbery Home School Poetry Residency, met John Dorsey in a burlesque-house in Milwaukee, and read at both of the legendary Kansas City Throwdown Poetry events. He is the co-founder and co-host of *Meet Me With Curiosity* Poetry In The Park at Klyde Warren Park in Dallas, Texas. He married the poet Reverie Evolving in a bookstore and dreams about cashews.

Benjamin Kuzemka is from suburban Chicago. He spent the first part of his twenties on a handful of continents and then joined a religious order. He left seminary, met a girl, and now lives in Saint Louis, Missouri. His first collection of poetry, *Dance Grooves for Gotikara,* will be released by Spartan Press in 2018.

W.E. Leathem lives and writes in Kansas City with his partner, son and her daughters. Founder and co-owner of Kansas City's Prospero's Books and Spartan Press. Leathem has published three books of poetry. His fourth, Glossolalia, will be released in 2018.

Gary Lechliter's work has recently appeared in many poetry journals and anthologies. He has published three full-length books of poetry. His newest book *Off the Beaten Path* is published by Woodley Press. Gary is the managing editor of *I-70 Review.*

Appointed the first Poet Laureate of Lucas County (2008-2014), by the Board of County Commissioners, Joel Lipman was raised in Kenosha, Wisconsin and has lived in Madison, Chicago, Buffalo and Toledo. Awarded Ohio's Governor's Award in 1988 and the 2011 Ohioana State Library's Pegasus Award for Lifetime Achievement, his poems are at https://www.poetryfoundation.org/poets/joel-lipman and currently in Inland Seas: Quarterly Journal of the National Museum of the Great Lakes (V73, Fall 2017, No.3).

Melvin Litton's stories have appeared in *Mobius, Foliate Oak, Floyd County Moonshine, Pif, Chiron Review, First Intensity,* with poetry in *Broadkill Review* and *The Stray Branch.* He has two published novels: *Geminga,* a man/raven fable concerning the Shining Path in Peru (III Publishing, 1993); and *I, Joaquin,* a fictional memoir of the Gold Rushbandit, Joaquin Murrieta, as told by his head encased in alcohol (Creative Arts Book Co., 2003) — both available in new editions from Crossroad Press. He is a retired carpenter and lives in Lawrence, KS with his wife Debra and their black and tan shepherd Jack. He also writes and performs songs solo and with the Border Band:www.borderband.com

Jim McGowin prefers to do art when he isn't stuck at his day job. He has been published a fair number of times online and in print, and has authored several chapbooks. He resides with his family and two cats in St. Louis, MO.

Jonie McIntire is the author of two chapbooks - *Not All Who Are Lost Wander,* (Finishing Line Press, 2016); and *Beyond the Sidewalk,* (NightBallet Press, 2017), Jonie McIntire has been active in the Toledo, Ohio poetry community for nearly twenty years. Jonie is a founding member of Toledo Poetry Museum, ToledoPoet.com and Almeda Street Poetry Co-op. Some of her publication credits include the online journal *Red Fez;* in the anthology *Sam & Andy's Uptown Café,* (Westron Press, 2001); as a regular contributor to the print journal *Khroma; in the Hessler Street Fair Anthology,* (Crisis Chronicles press, 2016); the anthology *Delirious,* (NightBallet Press, 2016); in online recordings for Lost Longe Gone Forgotten Records, (2017); and has even been stamped into cement as part of the Arts Commission of Greater Toledo's Sidewalk Poetry series. Her poem *Work Night* won 2nd place in the Toledo City Paper Poetry Contest in 2015 and her short poem *43612* won an honorable mention in 2017 Ode to the Zipcode contest. She is host to a number of monthly poetry reading series in Toledo and works with local non-profits to promote arts, education, and economic stability in Northwest Ohio.

Marybeth Niederkorn is a reporter for the Southeast Missourian newspaper in Cape Girardeau, and her fiction and poetry have appeared in *Trailer Park Quarterly, Small Town Tales anthology from Kapuha Press, Red Fez Entertainment,* and others. She holds a bachelor's degree in philosophy and a master's in professional writing from Southeast Missouri State University. She lives in southeast Missouri with her husband.

Shawn Pavey has delivered newspapers, mowed lawns, bagged groceries, cut meat, laid sewer pipe, bussed tables, washed dishes, roofed houses, crunched numbers, rented cars, worked in hotels, worn an apron at Kinko's, and been paid to write everything from résumés to music reviews. Currently, he earns a living as a Technical Recruiter in Mission, KS where he lives with his fiancée and two worthless but adorable cats. He is the author of *Talking to Shadows* (2008, Main Street Rag Press) and *Nobody Steals the Towels From a Motel 6* (2015, Spartan Press), Co-founder and former Associate Editor of *The Main Street Rag Literary Journal,* and a former board member and officer of The Writers Place, a Kansas

City-based literary non-profit. His poems, essays, and journalism appear in a variety of national and regional publications. He's hosted poetry readings in bars, coffee shops, haunted houses, bookstores, libraries, front porches, seedy motel rooms, and abandoned warehouses. A graduate of the University of North Carolina's Undergraduate Honors Creative Writing Program, he likes his Tom Waits loud, his bourbon single barrel, and his basketball Carolina Blue.

Americana songwriter and Kansas-City-based storyteller K.W. Peery is the author of five poetry collections: *Tales of a Receding Hairline; Purgatory; Wicked Rhythm; Ozark Howler; Gallatin Gallows. Tales of a Receding Hairline* was a semifinalist in the Goodreads Choice Awards – Best in Poetry 2016. Peery is a regular contributor in *Veterans Voices Magazine.* His work is included in the Vincent Van Gogh Anthology *Resurrection of a Sunflower* and the Walsall Poetry Society Anthology, *Diverse Verse II & III.*

Jeanette Powers is an anarchist poet and performance artist. Her work centers around *desyncopation* and battling the cage of habit. She also focuses on intersectional community development, with an eye towards justice and equality. She currently helps build the performative arts venue Uptown Arts Bar, lit-fest Fountainverse, the three-year KC based monthly publishing sequence Pop Poetry, EMP Books independent press, and the arts non-profit Chameleon. She's authored six published books of poetry, and is working on her third "practice novel". Her newest book, *Gasconade* is released in April 2018 by NightBallet Press. She is a fellow-resident at Osage Arts Community and can most often be found running creeks with her hound dog, Olly Moss.

Jamie Rhodes is an artist from Austin, Texas. Jamie's exhibition, *Shit I Can't Touch,* is about her experience being diagnosed with systemic nickel allergy syndrome 5 years ago and how she had to dramatically change her life in one day. After her diagnosis, she couldn't produce art and photography in the way she used to. She captures her experience with her diagnosis through various art forms. She has enjoyed several residences with OAC, her favorite was spending the summer photographing the Owens/Belle fair. In her past she's enjoyed painting, stained glass window making, creating chandeliers (permanent installation at the Belle warehouse), costume design, as well as teaching cooking classes and creating wedding cakes. She served on the board of Salvage Vanguard Theater for 5 years.

Stefene Russell is a poet and arts journalist in St. Louis, and the 2018 Laumeier Sculpture Park poet-in-residence. Her books include *Inferna* (2012, Intagliata Press), *The Possum Codex* (2015, Otis Nebula) and *Lararium* (2018, forthcoming, Spartan Press). Find out what she did last summer by reading her very sporadically updated blog at stefenerussell.com.

Kerry Trautman is a lifelong Ohioan, a founder/admin for ToledoPoet.com, and a poetry editor for *Red Fez.* Her poetry and fiction have appeared in several anthologies and journals such as *Slippery Elm, Free State Review, Midwestern Gothic, Hawaii Pacific Review*, and *Alimentum.* Her poetry chapbooks are *Things That Come in Boxes* (King Craft Press, 2012,) *To Have Hoped* (Finishing Line Press, 2015,) and *Artifacts* (NightBallet Press, 2017.)

Brett Lars Underwood is a bartender and a gadabout who writes, promotes and produces happenings and mishaps in St. Louis. Once upon a time, he co-published a 'zine entitled *Lick My Squaggle Noose, Clam Tick.* He penned Zen koans for *The Riverfront Times* and *St. Louis Magazine* as well as *Curator Magazine.* He has performed in backrooms, backyards, ballrooms, barrooms, basements, coffeehouses, courtyards, galleries, museums, rock venues and taverns. His verse and riddles have been published by *The Bicycle Review, 52nd City, The Subterranean, Bad Shoe* and included in *Flood Stage: An Anthology of Saint Louis Poets* and *The Gasconade Review presents 39 Feet And Rising.* He unleashed *Sunlit Insult,* his first chapbook, in 2011 and *Its Bush Lent Subtle Hints* in October, 2013. He can be reached at brettlarsunderwood@gmail.com

Jason M. Vaughn lives and writes in Basehor, KS. His work has appeared in various journals, including *Contrary, The Doctor T.J. Eckleburg Review, Slush Pile Magazine,* and *Monkeybicycle.* His screenplay, now titled *The Green Sea*, was a grand-prize winner in the 2012 Script Pipeline Screenwriting Competition.

K.S. Wuertz (Kim) was first published during her teenage years in *Bitterroot,* a national poetry journal in New York. In college, Kim's work was chosen for review during an Iowa writing symposium by Stephen Spender. Kim believes her background as an educator, social worker and her time in the ministry contributed to her decision to live her dream. In 2009, she became a full-time freelance writer. Since then, she's written (and illustrated) several books for children, competed her first novel series (*Life at Mimosa Lake*), begun an illustrated series about the pets in her life (*Souls and Paws*), written a stand-alone novel (*Soul Searching*) , several Christmas novellas (*Christmas at Mimosa Lake*), short stories and poems. Kim has 18 books in print with 2 more expected out by the end of the year. Kim is an award-winning author and illustrator, but also an editor and publisher. Her publishing company, KSWuertz Publications has published work for over 60 authors. She regularly writes for various devotional magazines and publications. Kim teaches writing workshops, judges writing contests and gives presentations to schools, churches, community groups and professional conferences about: her books, her life as a writer, and about the joy of living your dream!

Scot Young lives on a farm in the Ozark hills with his wife and a herd of goats. He is the publisher and editor of the Rusty Truck.

This book is dedicated to the memory of Murph.

This project was made possible, in part, by generous support from the Osage Arts Community.

Osage Arts Community provides temporary time, space and support for the creation of new artistic works in a retreat format, serving creative people of all kinds — visual artists, composers, poets, fiction and nonfiction writers. Located on a 152-acre farm in an isolated rural mountainside setting in Central Missouri and bordered by ¾ of a mile of the Gasconade River, OAC provides residencies to those working alone, as well as welcoming collaborative teams, offering living space and workspace in a country environment to emerging and mid-career artists. For more information, visit us at www.oac.com

www.ingramcontent.com/pod-product-compliance
Lightning Source LLC
Chambersburg PA
CBHW050615190726
48283CB00007B/2431

* 9 7 8 1 9 4 6 6 4 2 5 0 9 *